W9-BNP-083

# knit one,
# STRIPE TOO
## making the most of self-striping yarns

**Candace EISNER STRICK**

*Martingale®*
& COMPANY

Knit One, Stripe Too: Making the Most of Self-Striping
Yarns
© 2007 by Candace Eisner Strick

Martingale & Company
20205 144th Ave. NE
Woodinville, WA 98072-8478
www.martingale-pub.com

No part of this product may be reproduced in any
form, unless otherwise stated, in which case repro-
duction is limited to the use of the purchaser. The
written instructions, photographs, designs, projects, and patterns are intended for the personal,
noncommercial use of the retail purchaser and are
under federal copyright laws; they are not to be
reproduced by any electronic, mechanical, or other
means, including informational storage or retrieval
systems, for commercial use. Permission is granted to
photocopy patterns for the personal use of the retail
purchaser. Attention teachers: Martingale & Company
encourages you to use this book for teaching, subject
to the restrictions stated above.

The information in this book is presented in
good faith, but no warranty is given nor results
guaranteed. Since Martingale & Company has no
control over choice of materials or procedures, the
company assumes no responsibility for the use of this
information.

Printed in China
12 11 10 09 08 07     8 7 6 5 4 3 2 1

**Library of Congress Cataloging-in-Publication Data**
Library of Congress Control Number: 2007021897

ISBN: 978-1-56477-755-3

## CREDITS

President & CEO: Tom Wierzbicki
Publisher: Jane Hamada
Editorial Director: Mary V. Green
Managing Editor: Tina Cook
Technical Editor: Karen Costello Soltys
Copy Editor: Liz McGehee
Design Director: Stan Green
Assistant Design Director: Regina Girard
Illustrator: Adrienne Smitke
Cover & Text Designer: Shelly Garrison
Photographer: Brent Kane

## MISSION STATEMENT

Dedicated to providing quality products
and service to inspire creativity.

## DEDICATION

To the love of my life, Kenneth L. Strick. As promised, after five da capos, this is the fine.

## ACKNOWLEDGMENTS

Writing a book and working on more than 25 designs in a span of less than a year is a daunting task, to say the least. It overcomes your life, takes up every available waking hour, and sometimes even invades the sleeping hours. Thank you to all the people who have helped me along the way, not only for this particular book, but in my career in general as a knitwear designer, teacher, and author.

As always, my greatest gratitude goes to the wonderful people at Martingale & Company: Mary Green; Terry Martin; my editor, Karen Soltys; and all the other talented people who worked on this book.

I could not have written this book without the support of numerous people and yarn companies. Their generosity with yarns and getting them to me so quickly is very much appreciated. Thank you to Deanna Gavioli of Berroco; Randi Sunde and Melissa Parr of Norwegian Spirit; Joyce Rodriguez of Knit One, Crochet Too; Linda Pratt of Westminster Fibers; Katherine Cade of South West Trading Co.; Jean Lux of Universal Yarn; Linda Braley and Diana Harker of Skacel; Sara Arblaster of Patons; Nancy Thomas of Tahki/Stacy Charles; Lynn Lam of Yarn Place; Dave van Stralen of Louet; JoAnne Turcotte of Plymouth Yarn Co.; Barry Klein of Trendsetter; Laura Bryant of Prism; and Bev Galeskas of Fiber Trends. Thanks to Marilyn King of Black Water Abbey Yarns for beautiful buttons. Information about these yarns and buttons can be found in "Resources" on page 96.

Selma Kaplan and Diane Edington, who generously helped with the knitting for this book.

My friend Donna McLaughlin, who magically knows when I am overwhelmed, taking me away from the mounds of yarn and knitting and skillfully diverting my attention to fabric and quilting.

My Tuesday afternoon knit group: Linda Blum, Christiane Burkhard, Amy Chibeau, Diane Edington, Suzanne Murray, Monica Willding—thanks for the company and chocolate.

My travel mates, best friends, and most admired knitwear designers, Judy Pascale and Margaret Fisher; thanks for the laughs and good advice through all the time zones. I have learned so much from both of you.

Benjamin Bunny, one incredible little English angora rabbit who graced my life and ate my house for more than five years.

My mother and father, Sarah Greenspan Eisner and Raymond Eisner, who taught me everything I needed to know to make my life complete—music and the love of handicraft.

My sister, Judith Eisner, who most likely holds the world's record for sock knitting and who supports me no matter what I decide to do.

My three sons, Nathaniel, Liam, and Noah, who taught me the major requirement for my career: patience.

And Ken, my dear sweet husband, who makes up for everything and anything that goes wrong in my world. Without you, I would not be.

# CONTENTS

# INTRODUCTION

While writing this introduction, without leaving my computer chair, I could see stripes in over a dozen different places. The floorboards on my oak floor are striped due to the different color gradations of the pieces of wood; looking into my screened porch, I see a couch with striped cushions; the Raggedy Ann and Andy dolls in the corner of my studio sport red-and-white striped legs; I look down at the hand-knit striped socks I am wearing; the chipmunk in my garden has adorable little stripes up his back, and the ornamental striped grass in my front yard is about the only plant out there that I can grow. My neighbor's cat, strolling across my backyard looking for birds, sports jaunty orange stripes across his body, while the fat raccoon raiding my compost pile has a striped tail that Davy Crockett would covet.

Every post office and school in this country flies the American flag of stars and stripes. Go around the corner to the neighborhood barber shop and see the striped pole spinning its colors. Turn your TV on to watch a basketball game and see the referees decked out in their attire of vertically striped black-and-white shirts. Don't forget rugby shirts, too. In the grocery store, mall, and almost any store in the world, you will see bar codes on all the items for sale. Lay your head down at night on your pillow and recall the days when the best down pillows were covered in traditional blue-and-white ticking stripes. Chances are at least one upholstered piece of furniture in your house has stripes, not to mention rugs, blankets, sheets, curtains, and tablecloths.

Travel to Venice and see the handsome gondoliers in their traditional garb of horizontally striped black-and-white sweaters, while the mooring poles for their gondolas are bright blue-and-white stripes. Further south in Italy, the magnificent duomo in Orvieto is built in horizontal stripes of black-and-white marble. Travel on safari and see tigers and zebras. Visit a coral reef and see wildly striped and vivid tropical fish. End up in prison and you might be forced to wear stripes—horizontal ones at that!

Chances are you're heard the theory that horizontal stripes make one look fat, while vertical stripes make one look thin. I believe it to a certain extent, but please don't think this book is nothing but horizontal stripes and vertical stripes. There's more than one way of dealing with stripes, and taking perfectly gorgeous self-striping yarn and knitting a plain old stockinette-stitch sweater from bottom to top (not that it might not turn out extraordinarily beautiful) is not exactly what I had in mind. Sure, there's horizontal and there's vertical, but there are also diagonal, mitered, modular, and circular. There are also slip-stitch textures, using more than one yarn, and lots of other ways to work with stripes. Throw these in the mix with the magic yarn and you've got many interesting projects.

Stripes are definitely a bold statement, and they have been throughout history. Knitting stripes was

always popular, but now it has become effortlessly easy. About 10 years ago, when knitting socks became the rage (and still is, in fact!), yarn companies invented a nifty yarn that would actually make stripes all by itself. All you had to do was knit. With a minimum of effort, knitters were turning out impressively striped socks by the dozens. Judith Eisner, my sister who hadn't knit in more than 35 years, became excited about knitting again because of this yarn. This new invention was extremely important, as it kept knitters totally interested in knitting round and round on what was a rather uninteresting project, and it made them look like incredibly talented color experts to those people who didn't realize that the yarn did all of the color work. Like my sock-knitting friend Donna says about the self-striping yarn, "It makes me look really smart."

Dyed in certain lengths of color, this yarn was meant to be used to knit small-diameter items. It worked on socks, gloves, and very small items, but try to use it for anything bigger, and the stripes disappeared and turned into blobs. The next great invention for knitters was yarn that was dyed in really long runs of color. Now one could knit bigger items and still get the stripes that they craved. From pure wool to soy silk, corn silk, cotton, and synthetic, self-striping yarn is asserting itself in all weights, textures, and fiber content. The stripes are standing up and demanding to be noticed, both for their colors and textures.

When I started to contact yarn companies for yarn to use for this book, I was astounded by the array of self-striping yarns out there. One was more beautiful than the next, and the ideas invaded my head faster than my hands could knit the items. I wanted to use the yarn for everything, from traditional to funky, and I wanted to use it for things other than apparel. I wanted the knitter to have a fun experience, banishing all worrying details from the knitting. When Martingale asked me for more projects than I had proposed, little did they realize they had created a monster. And the monster desperately needed help. Enter my dear friend, Selma Kaplan. Truly we have to be sisters separated at birth, as she has been so intuitive to what I want that I find it impossible we do not share the same DNA. She is mathematically gifted and has a great sense of humor, pointing out all my stupid errors in a manner that encouraged me to continue. In my book, figuratively and literally, she is truly one of the world's greatest knitters. When I designed the Circles Stole/Scarf I was faced with needing dozens of circles and no time to knit them. To my rescue comes Diane Edington, my dear friend who lives yonder in a beautifully decorated and clean house that I covet. She cheerfully offered to help, and even after the required number of circles was completed, was still willing to keep going. Without Selma and Diane, this book would not have been possible.

So . . . prop up your feet, bring out the chocolate, get out your needles, and travel through the world of easy stripes. I hope you enjoy your trip.

# KNOW YOUR YARN

Browsing in a yarn store is perhaps one of my favorite pastimes. I often succumb to a beautiful skein and buy it on impulse, having not a clue what I will knit from it. Sometimes though, yarn in a skein isn't what we think. After many disappointments with multicolored yarn, I have learned my lesson. I now look long and carefully at the yarn, and I try to pry into its skein to see how long the lengths of colors are. The width of your knitting and the length of the color runs will determine what the finished product will look like.

## LENGTH OF COLOR RUNS

Not all yarns are created equal. If the label does not show a picture of what the yarn looks like when knit, or if your yarn shop hasn't displayed a knitted swatch of it, you'll then need to determine whether the yarn in question will stripe. If you want a self-striping yarn, you will need to see long lengths of color in the yarn. Ask the shop owner if you can pull out a very long length of the yarn from the ball and scrutinize the length of each color in the skein. Photograph A at right shows a yarn with short lengths of color, the longest being about 9", and the shortest being about 1½". Photograph B shows a skein with runs of color about 6½ yards or 234". Considering that one stitch, knit in sock-weight yarn on size 1 needles, uses about ¼" of yarn, while one stitch, knit in bulky-weight yarn on size 15 needles, uses about 1½" of yarn, the number of stitches you can knit from any one run of color varies a great deal. If the skein you are looking at has 3" to 4" of a color, your knitting won't be

striped unless you knit a three-stitch I-cord. If the skein has runs of color 6½ yards, as in photo B, then you will knit a definite stripe. How wide the stripe will be depends on how many stitches you are using.

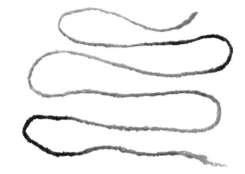

*A: Yarn with short runs of color*

*B: Yarn with long runs of color*

Conversely, if you use long runs of color in a small diameter, you'll create large blocks of color. This can be useful when working modularly, as entire sections can sometimes be one color. You create the look of using many skeins of yarn, with all the convenience of using only one skein.

Be careful when buying hand-dyed yarn. Sometimes the skein has been rewound after dyeing, making it somewhat difficult to determine the actual length of color runs. It is also hard to pull out a strand from a skein. Find where one color begins and try to trace its length along the skein until it changes into another color to determine the length of the color runs.

## FACTORY GLITCHES

Maddening but true, you will almost always find a knot or two, or even three, in the course of one skein. This is an unavoidable glitch that happens in the factory when the yarn breaks while being spun, or if the last skein is being made from the cone and there is not enough yarn left on the cone for a full skein. In the interests of economy, a knot is tied. If there were no knots in your skeins of yarn, chances are you'd be paying lots more money for them.

Adding insult to injury, the knot is sometimes tied to a totally different place in the order of the colors. I can imagine why this done, but for the life of me, I always think the person doing it must be color-blind. Whenever I find a knot in the skein, I cut it out and tie my own knot. Most knitting books say to start a new length of yarn at the side seam. This is sound advice. Do I always do it? No. When I find a knot that is tied to the wrong color of the series I pull out enough yarn until I find the place in the skein where I want to resume. I tie the knot, and I'm merrily back on course. After a few ungracious thoughts about the factory and its employees, I quickly forget it.

## DYE LOTS

Yarn like that shown at right is a great way to trick your best knitting friend. Ask him or her if the two skeins are the same dye lot. Remember to wager a skein of cashmere. Here is the answer: yes, the two skeins are the same dye lot. Self-striping yarn put up in balls can be somewhat of a mystery, as not only do the balls often look like totally different dye lots and even different colors, but sometimes the balls don't have every single color of the colorway in them. When I was knitting the Paint Box Stripes sweater on page 37, I had 14 skeins of yarn. In the skein some of them looked identical, but some didn't. Upon closer inspection, I found entire skeins that didn't have the same colors in them as other skeins. So a lot depends on how many different colors are in the colorway, the length of the particular colors within that colorway, and how many yards are wound into each skein. After knitting the Paint Box Stripes sweater, I decided that it might be a good idea to buy an extra skein or two of yarn for a project, just in case you want to do closer matching. I'll talk about that a little later.

And here's something else just to make you a little more crazy: starting the ball from the center (if it's a pull skein), or from the outside, can make the colors stripe in opposite order. For instance, if the colors in the progression make stripes that go from red to blue to yellow to green, then start over again, starting the ball from the opposite end will make stripes that run from green to yellow to blue to red. If the progression of color is totally symmetrical, such as red to blue to yellow to blue to red, then it will not matter which end you start. If you don't care at all about matching, then you have read this paragraph for nothing.

## MATCHING

To match or not to match, that is a personal decision. There are two camps of sock knitters, those who go to great lengths to get identical twin socks, and those who don't care a hoot and start the second sock at any point in the color run. I am one of those who doesn't care if my socks match, but am more likely to go to greater lengths to match something that will be on my body in a place where most people's eyes rest, such as the two sides of a sweater by the front neck shaping. These two shoulder sides of the piece are worked either separately or at the same time with two skeins of yarn. I would be more inclined to believe that these two sides should match. If matching doesn't matter to you, then you are free to knit them from wherever you are in the skein of yarn.

Matching also becomes a dilemma if one knits in the round, breaks for the armholes, then resumes the knitting by working back and forth. Knitting the lower part of the sweater in the round will produce stripes that are narrower than those produced when working back and forth. If your yarn is striping with huge contrast, then you might want to knit everything flat. If the yarn is more subtle, flowing from one color to the next without sharp contrast, then you might get away with working the piece both ways. I have decided that I like the more even look of working each piece back and forth. If you work in this manner, matching the side seams becomes something that requires a decision. I decided to not match stripes at my side seams, beginning each piece wherever I happened to be in the skein.

What about when you run out of one skein and have to attach a new skein? Should you search for the place in the skein that has the same color and tie it in

there? Only if you want to. For the Paint Box Stripes, which features cuff-to-cuff construction, I searched for the place in the ball that was the same color as where I left off. Because the yarn used for that sweater gradually faded from one color to the next rather than creating a sharp change of color, I felt this method would look much better. When knitting a project where you plan to match color runs from one skein to the next, you'd benefit from having a few extra skeins on hand. For the other projects, I was mindful of where I was in the color run when attaching the new yarn, but not fanatic about it.

## IT'S NOT ROCKET SCIENCE

One of the nice things about self-striping yarn is that you don't have to make the color changes yourself; the yarn does it for you. It's up to you to decide how much control you want over the yarn. While some yarns are very predictable with consistent color lengths, sometimes a glitch causes a color to fall slightly short of its previous lengths. To me, this adds some extra fun and interest. If someone points it out to me and insinuates that I made a mistake, I can just place the blame on the yarn.

## THE MYSTERY REVEALED (SORT OF)

My husband built a dye studio for me, and I have spent many long, happy hours in it, producing many beautiful and some not-so-beautiful skeins.

I have pondered how I would go about dyeing a skein with very long runs of color. Most yarns are put up in skeins of roughly 60" circumference. If I wanted to dye a skein into self-striping yarn using two colors, I'd dye half of the skein, or 30", in color A, and the other half in color B. That would give me runs of color less than a yard long, which is sufficient to stripe about one round in a medium-sized sock. If I wanted longer runs, I'd have to rewind to a much longer length. It can be done in a home studio, but it's tedious.

I have known people who put wooden stakes in the ground very far apart, then rewind the yarn around them. Some people use their fence posts. This gives them a longer skein and they can then apply the colors at longer lengths. The problem arises when you try to process the skein with heat. You somehow have to coil it all up and keep the various colors from running into each other. I have also read of people who have pulled out the desired length of yarn they want for one color, paint the dye on, coil that one section all up, proceed with the next color, and so on. Maybe a somewhat easier method is to knit a large sheet of fabric on the knitting machine, paint the dye onto this fabric in stripes, process the fabric, ravel it out, wind it into skeins, and then knit the desired garment. After getting tired just thinking about it, I decided to let a factory do it all for me!

While working with the Paint Box yarn (see the project on page 37), I watched as the colors blended from one to the other, making an intermediate color as they blended. I surmised that this yarn was dyed in the wool. In other words, the roving was first dyed, then spun into yarn. After talking to Hélène Rush of Knit One, Crochet Too, I learned that this process is called *rainbow dyeing*. The fibers are first dyed, then spun. After dyeing certain lengths of one color, a new color is introduced in small amounts, then gradually added more and more until the roving is 100% of the second color. When the yarn is spun, the color gradually blends from one to the other, making subtle intermediate colors in the transition.

The striped yarn I used in the Basket Weave Pullover (page 33) was different from the Paint Box yarn. This yarn went abruptly from one color to the next without any transition, producing a garment with clean crisp stripes. Barry Klein, owner of Trendsetter Yarns, told me how this was achieved. This yarn, like the Paint Box yarn, is also made by first dyeing the fiber and then spinning it. However, when the colors are changed in the Trendsetter yarn, there is no overlap, so one color goes directly into the next.

The Pandora yarn I used for the Softly Striping Ruana (page 57) is made from different textures of nylon to create the ribbon, pom-pom, and lash sections. Predetermined lengths of each type of nylon are programmed into a computer, and then each kind of nylon is put on a chain base by specialized machinery. After the spinning is completed, the yarn is wound into skeins. When dyed, each kind of nylon takes the dye a little differently. When knit, the yarn stripes both in color and texture.

The Suede yarn used in the skirt on page 54 also jumped from one color to the next without an intermediate color. Margery Winter, creative director of Berroco, explained the process to me. A single strand of nylon is dyed into predetermined lengths. These strands are then woven on a very narrow loom with a computer controlling the lengths of each color. The BoHo yarn I used in the Texture Striping Skirt (page 51) is made from several different fibers, each one predyed. The spinning machine spins each length, joining one into the next at different intervals.

Considering all the beautiful yarns I had to work with, the choice of letting the factory make it for me was a good one.

Geometry is infinitely interesting to knit, so it stands to reason that a baby would be thrilled to look at it. This blanket is composed of four mitered squares. When you use two different yarns that stripe, mathematically speaking, you get stripes$^2$—stripes to the second power.

Skill Level: Intermediate ■■■□

## FINISHED MEASUREMENTS

**Blanket:** 34" x 34"

**Each square:** 17" x 17"

## MATERIALS

Foliage by Berroco (53% new wool/47% acrylic; 1¾ oz/50 g; 100 yds/92 m) (4)

**A:** 6 skeins of color 5933, Carnation (pastels)

**B:** 6 skeins of color 5990, Batchelor Button (blues/purples)

US 11 (8 mm) needles or size needed to obtain gauge

K/10½ (6.5 mm) crochet hook

## GAUGE

13 sts and 26 rows = 4" in garter stitch

## SPECIAL ABBREVIATIONS

**CD (central decrease):** Sl 2 sts tog kw, K1, pass slipped sts tog as a unit over the K1.

**CE (chain edge):** Wyif sl 1 pw, return yarn to back of work between needles.

## GARTER STITCH

Knit every row.

## BLANKET

**Square 1:** Using A, CO 110 sts.

　**Row 1(WS):** CE, K53, P2tog, K54—109 sts.

　**Row 2:** CE, K52, CD, K53.

　**Row 3:** CE, K52, P1 (the middle st resulting from CD), K53.

Following the chart on page 14 for row/color sequence, cont in above manner until 3 sts rem. Work CD. Fasten off.

**Square 2:** Work as for square 1.

**Square 3:** Using A, PU 55 sts along top edge of square 2 and 55 sts along RS of square 1. (Refer to schematic below for placement of squares 1 and 2.) Work as for square 1.

**Square 4:** PU 55 sts along bottom of square 1 and 55 sts along left side of square 2. Work as for square 1.

## FINISHING

With A, sc all around perimeter of blanket, working 3 scs in each corner.

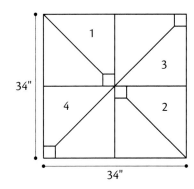

| MITERED BABY BLANKET COLOR SEQUENCE | | |
|:---:|:---:|:---:|
| **Number of Rows to Work** | **Color** | **Number of Sts Each Side of Center St*** |
| CO | A | |
| 3 | A | 53 |
| 4 | B | 51 |
| 2 | A | 50 |
| 6 | B | 47 |
| 2 | A | 46 |
| 2 | B | 45 |
| 4 | A | 43 |
| 4 | B | 41 |
| 2 | A | 40 |
| 6 | B | 37 |
| 4 | A | 35 |
| 2 | B | 34 |
| 2 | A | 33 |
| 8 | B | 29 |
| 4 | A | 27 |
| 2 | B | 26 |
| 6 | A | 23 |
| 2 | B | 22 |
| 4 | A | 20 |
| 8 | B | 16 |
| 2 | A | 15 |
| 2 | B | 14 |
| 8 | A | 10 |
| remainder | B | |
| *Number of stitches listed is the number remaining after the last row of that particular color has been worked.* | | |

**P**retty in pink, perfect princess, party pinafore . . . the trite, alliterative descriptions can go on and on to describe this cute little jumper. Suffice it to say, it's easy to knit and has just the right amount of feminine frill.

Skill Level: Easy ■■□□

## FINISHED MEASUREMENTS

**To fit size:** 2 (4, 6) years

**Chest:** 22 (24, 26)"

**Length:** 20 (21, 22)"

**Armhole depth:** 5 (5½, 6)"

**Lower circumference:** 37 (41, 45)"

## MATERIALS

3 (4, 4) skeins of Classic Worsted LP by Universal Yarn Inc. (80% acrylic/20% wool; 3½ oz /100 g; 197 yds/180 m), color 9728 (pink stripes) (4)

US 9 (5.5 mm) needles or size required to obtain gauge

G/6 (4.25 mm) crochet hook

## GAUGE

16 sts and 20 rows = 4" in St st

## SMOCKING STITCH

(Multiple of 8 + 2 sts)

**Row 1 and all WS rows:** K2, *P2, K2, rep from * to end.

**Row 2:** P2, *K2, P2, rep from * to end.

**Row 4:** P2, *wyib insert RH needle from front between 6th and 7th sts on LH needle and draw through a lp, sl this lp onto LH needle and knit it tog with first st, K1, P2, K2, P2*, rep from * to * to end.

**Row 6:** Work as for row 2.

**Row 8:** P2, K2, P2, *wyib draw lp as before from front between 6th and 7th sts and knit it tog with first st, K1, P2, K2, P2*, rep from * to * to last 4 sts, K2, P2.

Rep these 8 rows for patt.

## FRONT

Picot CO as foll: cable-edge CO 4 sts (see page 92), *BO 2 sts, sl st from RH needle kw to LH needle, cable-edge CO 4 sts*, rep from * to * 37 (41, 45) times, ending last rep when st on RH is slipped back to LH needle—37 (41, 45) picots made—74 (82, 90) sts.

Knit 6 rows.

Work in St st until piece measures 12 (13, 14)", ending with a completed WS row.

Work 13 rows of smocking st.

**Shape armholes:** BO 8 sts at beg of next 2 rows—58 (66, 74) sts.

Work even in patt until armhole measures 3 (3½, 4)", ending with a completed row 5 or row 1.

**Shape neck (RS):** Work 14 (18, 22) sts; BO middle 30 sts kw, working each set of P2 sts tog as 1 st; work rem 14 sts.

**Straps:** Work each strap in smocking st as established for 2", ending with a completed WS row.

Join shoulders using 3-needle BO (see page 92), working the purl sts tog as 1 st.

## BACK

Work as for front.

## FINISHING

Beg at shoulder, work sc around neck, working 2 sc in each corner.

Sew side seams. Sc around armholes.

This dress needs no blocking. Do not iron, as the acrylic in the yarn will lose its body.

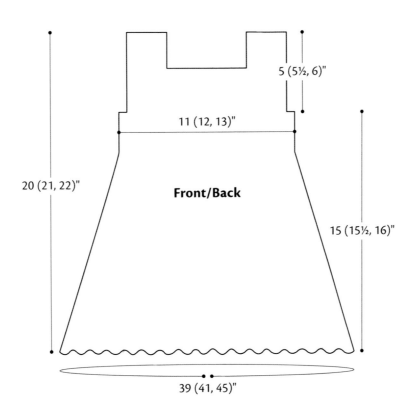

5 (5½, 6)"

11 (12, 13)"

20 (21, 22)"

**Front/Back**

15 (15½, 16)"

39 (41, 45)"

**M**y mother used to sing this rather violent song to me as a lullaby—"Bye baby bunting, daddy's gone a-hunting, to catch a little rabbit skin to wrap his baby bunting in." Let the bunny live and keep his fur! Knit the bunting from soft and pretty striped yarn.

Skill Level: Intermediate ■■■□

## FINISHED MEASUREMENTS

**To fit sizes:** newborn (3 months, 6 months)

**Width:** 22 (24½, 27)"

**Length to armhole:** 18 (19, 20)"

**Armhole depth:** 5 (5, 5)"

**Sleeve Length:** 7 (7½, 8)"

## MATERIALS

3 skeins of Classic Worsted LP by Universal Yarn Inc. (80% acrylic/20% wool; 3½ oz/100 g; 197 yds/180 m), color 9611 (blue stripes) **4**

US 9 (5.5 mm) needles or size needed to obtain gauge

US 7 (4.5 mm) needles

20" zipper

## GAUGE

19½ sts and 26 rows = 4" in diagonal patt on larger needles

## DIAGONAL PATTERN FOR BACK, RIGHT FRONT, AND SLEEVES

(Multiple of 6 sts)

**Row 1 (RS):** *K4, P2, rep from * to end.

**Row 2:** *K2, P4, rep from * to end.

**Row 3:** Work as for row 1.

**Row 4:** Work as for row 2.

**Row 5:** K2, *P2, K4*, rep from * to * to last 4 sts, P2, K2.

**Row 6:** P2, *K2, P4*, rep from * to * to last 4 sts, K2, P2.

**Row 7:** Work as for row 5.

**Row 8:** Work as for row 6.

**Row 9:** *P2, K4, rep from * to end.

**Row 10:** *P4, K2, rep from * to end.

**Row 11:** Work as for row 9.

**Row 12:** Work as for row 10.

Rep these 12 rows for patt.

## DIAGONAL PATTERN FOR LEFT FRONT

(Multiple of 6)

**Row 1 (RS):** *K4, P2, rep from * to end.

**Row 2:** *K2, P4, rep from * to end.

**Rows 3 and 4:** Rep rows 1 and 2.

**Row 5:** *P2, K4, rep from * to end.

**Row 6:** *K2, P4, rep from * to end.

**Rows 7 and 8:** Rep rows 5 and 6.

**Row 9:** K2, *P2, K4*, rep from * to * to last 4 sts, P2, K2.

**Row 10:** P2, *K2, P4*, rep from * to * to last 4 sts, K2, P2.

**Rows 11 and 12:** Rep rows 9 and 10.

Rep these 12 rows for patt.

## BACK

CO 54 (60, 66) sts with smaller needles.

Knit 9 rows.

Change to larger needles. Work in patt until piece measures 18 (19, 20)", ending with a completed WS row.

**Shape armhole:** BO 5 sts at beg of next 2 rows—44 (50, 56) sts.

Work even in patt until armhole measures 4", ending with a completed WS row.

**Shape shoulders:** BO 5 (6, 7) sts at beg of next 2 rows—34 (38, 42) sts. BO 5 sts at beg of next 4 rows. BO rem 14 (18, 22) sts.

## RIGHT FRONT

CO 30 (30, 36) sts with smaller needles.

Knit 9 rows.

Change to larger needles. Work in patt, working first 6 sts of every RS row and last 6 sts of every WS row in garter st.

Work until piece measures 18 (19, 20)", ending with a completed RS row.

**Shape armhole:** Cont to keep first 6 sts next to front opening in garter st. BO 5 sts at beg of next WS row—25 (25, 31) sts.

Work even in patt until armhole measures 1½ (2, 2½)", ending with a completed WS row.

**Shape neck:** BO 4 sts at beg of next RS row, 2 sts at beg of next RS row, 1 (1, 2) sts at beg of next RS row, 1 st at beg of next 2 RS rows—17 (16, 21) sts. Work even until armhole measures same as back, ending with a completed RS row.

**Shape shoulder:** BO 5 (6, 7) sts at beg of next WS row, BO 6 (5, 7) sts at beg of next 2 WS rows.

## LEFT FRONT

Use patt st for left front. Work as for right front, reversing all directions and keeping 6 sts of garter st at front edge opening.

## SLEEVES

CO 32 sts with smaller needles.

Knit 8 rows. Knit 1 more row, inc 10 sts evenly spaced—42 sts.

Change to larger needles and work in diagonal patt until piece measures 7 (7½, 8)" from beg, ending with a completed WS row. BO all sts.

## FINISHING

Sew left and right fronts to back at shoulder seams.

With smaller needle, RS facing, and starting at right front center, PU 46 sts around neck opening. Knit 8 rows. BO all sts loosely.

Sew sleeves into armhole openings; sew sleeve and side seams. Sew bottom seam. Sew in zipper.

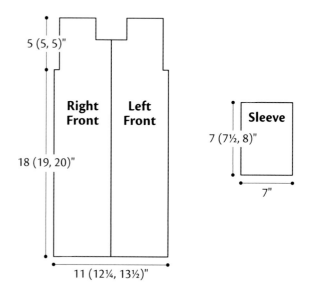

Yes, you can dance all night, but maybe you'd just get tired and want to go to bed. Better yet, you can wear these socks at dance class. They will keep your ankles and insteps warm, but you won't slip and fall.

**Skill Level:** Intermediate ◼◼◼◻

## FINISHED MEASUREMENTS

**To fit size:** Women's medium

**Circumference:** 9"

**Leg length:** 7"

**Foot length:** 2½"

## MATERIALS

2 skeins of Regia 6-ply Crazy Color (75% new wool/25% polyamide; 1¾ oz/50 g; 135 yds/125 m), color 5260 (bright blues and yellow) ❸

US 5 (3.75 mm) double-pointed needles or size needed to obtain gauge

## GAUGE

21½ sts = 4" in slip-stitch rib patt

## SLIP-STITCH RIB PATTERN

**Rnd 1:** *K1, wyif sl 1 st pw, return yarn to back of work, rep from * to end of rnd.

**Rnd 2:** Knit.

Rep these 2 rnds for patt.

## GARTER STITCH IN THE ROUND

**Rnd 1:** Purl.

**Rnd 2:** Knit.

Rep these 2 rnds for patt.

## SOCK

*Make 2 exactly alike.*

CO 48 sts. Distribute sts evenly on 3 needles (16 sts on each). Join rnd, being careful not to twist sts.

Work slip-stitch rib patt for 7", ending with a completed rnd 2.

**Divide for heel:**

> **Rnd 1:** Work 20 sts in slip-stitch rib patt, BO next 28 sts. Work 20 sts in slip-stitch rib patt, cable CO 28 sts.

> **Rnds 2–5:** Work 20 sts in slip-stitch rib patt, work rem 28 sts in garter st.

Work all sts in slip-stitch rib patt until foot measures 2½".

Work 5 rnds of garter st. BO all sts.

## RUFFLE

PU 48 sts around top CO edge of leg.

**Rnd 1:** Knit.

**Rnd 2:** *K1, kfb, rep from * around.

**Rnd 3:** Knit.

**Rnd 4:** Kfb in every st.

**Rnd 5:** Knit.

BO all sts.

## FINISHING

Weave in all loose ends.

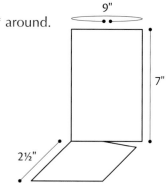

I like to wear bright and fun things on my hands and feet. Adding beads to your knitting dresses up the mitts even more and opens up whole new buying possibilities.

23

Skill Level: Intermediate ◼◼◼◻

## FINISHED MEASUREMENTS

**To fit size:** Women's Medium

**Circumference:** 8½"

**Length:** 6½"

## MATERIALS

2 skeins of Regia 6-ply Crazy Color (75% new wool/25% polyamide; 1¾ oz/50 g; 135 yds/125 m), color 5404 (bright orange/purple/green) ③

US 3 (3.25 mm) double-pointed needles or size needed to obtain gauge

US 1 (2.25 mm) double-pointed needles

1.25 mm crochet hook

196 seed beads, size 6/0

Stitch markers

## GAUGE

26 sts and 39 rows = 4" in St st with larger needles

## STOCKINETTE STITCH IN THE ROUND

Knit every round.

## BEADED RIBBING

(Multiple of 4 sts)

**Rnd 1:** *P3, K1, rep from * around.

**Rnd 2:** *P3, wyib sl 1 st pw, rep from * around.

**Rnd 3:** *P3, place bead on sl st wyib as foll: insert crochet hook through center of bead, slide hook into sl st and pull st through bead center; place st on RH needle (do not work st!), rep from * around.

**Rnd 4:** *P3, wyib sl 1 st pw, rep from * around.

## MITTS

*Make 2 exactly alike.*

With larger needles, CO 56 sts. Join, being careful not to twist sts, and pm.

Work the beaded ribbing patt 7 times. Work rnd 1 once more.

Knit 1 rnd.

**Beg thumb gusset:**

> **Rnd 1:** Kfb, kfb, pm; knit rem sts of rnd—4 thumb sts.
>
> **Rnd 2:** Knit.
>
> **Rnd 3:** Kfb, knit to 1 st before thumb-gusset marker, kfb; knit rem sts of rnd—6 thumb sts.
>
> **Rnd 4:** Knit.

Work rnds 3 and 4 until there are 16 sts for thumb gusset, ending with a completed rnd 4.

Place 16 thumb sts on a waste yarn. CO 2 sts.

Knit 16 rnds.

Change to smaller needles; purl 6 rnds. BO.

**Thumb:** Transfer 16 thumb sts from waste yarn to larger needles. PU 3 sts along back side of thumb opening—19 sts; distribute sts onto 3 needles. Knit 6 rnds. Change to smaller needles. Purl 6 rnds. BO.

## FINISHING

Weave in all loose ends.

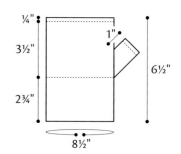

**Y**ou'll have a good laugh when you finish knitting these slippers, as they look like they would fit Paul Bunyan. Beware! Once they go into the washer for felting, you'll need to check them every few minutes so they won't shrink too much. In no time at all, you'll be joyfully and colorfully padding around the house in them.

Skill Level: Intermediate ◼◼◼▢

## FINISHED MEASUREMENTS AFTER FELTING

**To fit size:** Adult Medium

**Sole length:** 10"

**Height from sole to fringe:** 7"

## MATERIALS

**A:** 2 skeins of Fritidsgarn from Spirit of Norway (100% wool; 1¾ oz/50 g; 76 yds/70 m), color 9367 (turquoise jacquard striping) (5)

**B:** 1 skein of Fritidsgarn from Spirit of Norway, color 3937 (rust) (5)

US 13 (9 mm) needles or size needed to obtain gauge

US 13 (9 mm) double-pointed needles

Stitch markers

## GAUGE

12 sts and 16 rows = 4" in St st

## GARTER STITCH

Knit every row.

## STOCKINETTE STITCH

Knit the RS rows; purl the WS rows.

## SLIPPER SOLE

With B and single-pointed needles, CO 24 sts, pm, CO 2 sts, pm, CO 24 sts—50 sts. Knit 2 rows.

**Row 1:** K1, M1, knit to marker, M1, K2 between markers, M1, knit to last st, M1, K1.

**Row 2:** Knit.

Work the previous 2 rows 4 more times—70 sts.

Change to A and, starting with a knit row, work in St st for 12 rows.

## INSTEP

**Row 1:** K37, sl 1 kw, K1, psso, K1, turn. You can safely remove both markers now.

**Row 2:** Sl 1 pw, P5, P2tog, P1, turn.

**Row 3:** Sl 1 pw, knit to 1 st from gap, sl 1 kw, K1, psso, K1, turn.

**Row 4:** Sl 1 pw, purl to 1 st from gap, P2tog, P1, turn.

Rep rows 3 and 4 until 14 sts rem on each side of short rows.

**Next row:** Sl 1 pw, knit across all sts in row, closing the gap.

**Next row:** Purl across all sts in row, closing the gap—50 sts.

Work even in St st for 16 rows.

**Eyelet row:** K1, *K2tog, YO, rep from * to last st, K1.

Work 10 rows of garter st, inc 2 sts evenly spaced on last row—52 sts.

## I-CORD FRINGE

Using dpns, work first 4 sts in I-cord. To create I-cord, K4, slide the sts to the other end of the dpn and knit again. Do not turn between rows. Work until I-cord measures 2".

**Next row:** K2tog twice.

**Next row:** K2tog and fasten off.

Fasten yarn to next set of 4 sts, work I-cord as above. Cont making I-cord fringe with each set of 4 sts. Weave in all ends when done.

## FINISHING

Turn down garter-st top and tack in a few places to hold.

Sew back seam and sole seam.

Using A, make two 4-st I-cord ties, each 36" long, to thread through eyelet row (make long enough to tie in a bow.

Felt the slippers, referring to "Felting" on page 90.

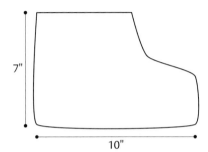

7"

10"

Traditional Shetland scarves are sometimes striped by using different shades of yarn. I went one step past tradition and carried a thin strand of mohair along with the self-striping yarn. The effect is soft and beautiful. Try making it short as a neck cozy (shown), or knit a narrow, longer model.

Skill Level: Intermediate ◼◼◼◻

## FINISHED MEASUREMENTS

9" x 29", unblocked

*If you wish to make a narrower scarf that is longer, follow directions in ( ).*

## MATERIALS

**A:** 2 skeins of Sisu Fantasy from Spirit of Norway (80% wool/20% nylon; 1¾ oz/50 g; 175yds/160 m), color 9367 (turquoise jacquard striping) 🧶2

**B:** 1 skein of Douceur et Soie from Knit One, Crochet Too (70% baby mohair/30% silk; ¾ oz/25 g; 225 yds/205 m), color 8512 (turquoise) 🧶2

US 5 (3.75 mm) needles or size needed to obtain gauge

## GAUGE

25 sts and 28 rows = 4" worked in razor shell patt, holding A and B tog.

## SPECIAL ABBREVIATIONS

**CE (chain edge):** Wyif sl 1 pw, return yarn to back between needles.

## RAZOR SHELL PATTERN

(Multiple of 10 + 5 sts)

**Row 1 (RS):** CE, K1, K2tog, *K3, YO, K1, YO, K3, K3tog*, rep from * to * to last 11 sts, K3, YO, K1, YO, K3, K2tog, K2.

**Row 2 (WS):** CE, knit.

## SCARF

CO 65 (35) sts using both yarns held tog.

Work in razor shell patt until yarn has nearly run out, ending on a completed row 1. Leave just enough to BO (about 4 times the width of your scarf).

BO kw from WS.

*Note:* To keep the striped yarn colors in sequence, end the first ball at the end of a color run and start the second ball at the beginning of the next color run. To avoid disrupting the chain edge, add the new skein of yarn in the middle of a row and weave in ends.

Block if desired.

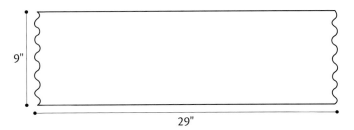

Pretty swirls and blocks of color are produced when you use short rows to create the top of this hat. Jazz it up with a curlicue or pretty buttons.

Skill Level: Experienced ●■■▬

## FINISHED MEASUREMENTS

**To fit size:** Women's Medium

**Circumference:** 22"

**Top diameter:** 8½"

**Side depth:** 4½"

## MATERIALS

2 skeins of Berroco Foliage (53% new wool/ 47% acrylic; 1¾ oz/50 g; 100 yds/92 m), color 5933, Carnation (pastels) (4)

US 9 (5.5 mm) 16" circular needle or size needed to obtain gauge

## GAUGE

16 sts and 20 rnds = 4" in St st

## GARTER STITCH

Knit every row.

## STOCKINETTE STITCH IN THE ROUND

Knit every round.

## SPECIAL ABBREVIATIONS

**CE (chain edge):** Wyif sl 1 pw, return yarn to back of work between needles.

## HAT TOP

The circle for the top of the hat is worked in garter st using short rows. For more details and illustrations on working short rows (making the wraps, turning, and hiding the wraps), see "Short-Row Shaping" on page 92.

CO 19 sts.

**Row 1 (WS):** Wyib sl 1 st kw, knit to end of row.

**Row 2:** CE, knit to 2 sts before end of row, wrap next st as follows: Bring yarn to front, sl st pw, bring yarn to back. Turn work (yarn is in front), sl the wrapped st pw to RH needle, knit to end of row.

**Row 3:** CE, knit to last 3 sts, wrap and turn as in row 2 and work back.

**Row 4:** CE, knit to last 4 sts, wrap and turn as in row 2 and work back.

Cont, wrapping and turning 1 st earlier each row.

Work until last row is: CE, K2, wrap and turn, knit back.

Final row of section will hide the wraps; it is a RS row: CE, K2, insert needle into wrap from bottom to top, slide it over st on LH needle, knit both st and wrap tog tbl. Cont across row. The first section is complete.

Work 5 more sections as above.

Attach last row of last section with live sts to first row of first section, sewing live sts to CO row.

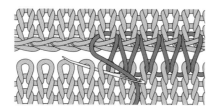

## UPPER BAND

The upper band is worked in St st from WS to produce rev St st from RS.

With RS facing, PU 96 sts around outside of circle, 1 st in each CE. Exchange places with first and last st to join. Turn work so WS is facing. Knit 7 rnds. BO all sts.

## HAT BODY

The hat body is worked in St st.

With RS of hat facing and rev St st unrolled so that St st side of roll is facing, PU 96 sts, 1 st in each CE.

**Rnd 1:** Knit.

**Rnd 2:** *K10, K2tog, rep from * around—88 sts.

**Rnds 3–13:** Knit.

**Rnd 14:** *K9, K2tog, rep from * around—80 sts.

**Rnds 15–20:** Knit.

**Rnd 16:** *K8, K2tog, rep from * around—72 sts.

**Rnd 17:** Knit.

## LOWER BAND

The lower band is worked in St st from WS to produce rev St st from RS.

Turn work to WS. Exchange places of first and last st. Knit 7 rnds. BO loosely.

## CURLICUE

*Make 2.*

CO 12 sts. Knit into front, back, and then front of each st—36 sts. BO.

## FINISHING

At one spot, bring upper band to meet lower band and sew curlicue through all layers to hold bands together.

Sew remaining curlicue to top of hat.

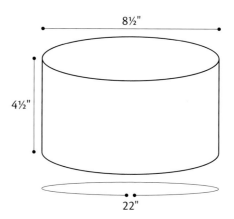

**W**eave a world of color and texture by using only two colors in any one row. The two different tones of striping yarn create a masterpiece that looks far more complicated than it really is. Thick, cushy, and soft, this sweater will be a favorite for cozy weekends, quiet nights by the fire, and long walks on the beach. Oops—almost forgot—also candlelit dinners.

Skill Level: Intermediate ◼◼◼◻

## FINISHED MEASUREMENTS

**Bust:** 38 (41, 43½, 46, 49)"

**Length:** 23 (23, 25½, 26, 28¼)"

**Sleeve length to underarm:** 20 (21, 21, 21, 21¼)"

## MATERIALS

Stripe by Lane Borgosesia/Trendsetter Yarns (100% wool; 3½ oz/100 g; 154 yds/140 m):

    **A (light):** 4 (4, 5, 5, 6) skeins of color 1660, Cotton Willow (cream/tan/gray) 🔵4️⃣

    **B (dark):** 6 (6, 7, 7, 8) skeins of color 1664, Harvest (rust/brown) 🔵4️⃣

US 9 (5.5 mm) needles or size needed to obtain gauge

US 7 (4.5 mm) needles

US 7 (4.5 mm) 16" circular needle

Stitch holders

Stitch markers

## GAUGE

17¼ sts and 36 rows = 4" in basket weave patt with larger needles

16 sts and 19 rows = 4" in St st

## BASKET WEAVE PATTERN

(Multiple of 6 + 4 sts)

**Foundation row (WS):** With B (dark), purl.

**Row 1 (light):** K4, *sl 2 wyib, K4, rep from * to end.

**Row 2 (light):** P1, K3, *sl 2 wyif, K4, rep from * to last 6 sts, sl 2, K3, P1.

**Row 3 (light):** Work as for row 1.

**Row 4 (light):** Work as for row 2.

**Row 5 (dark):** Knit.

**Row 6 (dark):** Purl.

**Row 7 (light):** K1, *sl 2 wyib, K4, rep from * to last 3 sts, sl 2, K1.

**Row 8 (light):** P1, *sl 2 wyif, K4, rep from * to last 3 sts, sl 2, P1.

**Row 9 (light):** Work as for row 7.

**Row 10 (light):** Work as for row 8.

**Row 11 (dark):** Knit.

**Row 12 (dark):** Purl.

Rep rows 1–12 for patt.

## BACK

For the border, using smaller needles and A, CO 82 (88, 94, 100, 106) sts.

Knit 4 rows.

Change to larger needles.

Work the 12-row basket weave patt 3 times, beg with foundation row and reversing colors (light for dark; dark for light). Work the foll 2 rows with A:

**RS:** Purl.

**WS:** Knit.

Knit 1 row with B to complete border.

For the main part of the back, beg with foundation row and using colors indicated, work the 12-row patt rep 8 (8, 9, 9, 10) times. Work rows 1–10 once more.

**Shape armholes (patt rows 11 and 12):** BO 12 sts at beg of next 2 rows—58 (64, 70, 76, 82) sts.

Work 12-row patt rep 5 (5, 5, 6, 6) times. Work rows 1–4 (1–4, 1–10, 1–4, 1–10) once more.

**Shape back neck on row 5 (5, 11, 5, 11):** Work 19 (21, 23, 25, 27) sts, place middle 20 (22, 24, 26, 28) sts on a holder for back neck.

**Right shoulder:** Work patt through row 11 (11, 5, 11, 5).

Place 19 (21, 23, 25, 27) sts on holder for shoulder.

**Left shoulder:** Attach yarn at neck edge and work as for right shoulder.

## FRONT

Work as for back through armhole shaping.

Work the 12-row patt rep 3 (3, 3, 3, 4) times. Work rows 1–5 (1–5, 1–11, 1–11, 1–5) once more.

**Shape neck on row 6 (6, 12, 12, 6):** P24 (27, 30, 32, 35), purl next 10 (10, 10, 12, 12) sts and place on holder for front neck, P24 (27, 30, 32, 35).

Work each side separately.

**Left shoulder:** Work next row even in patt. Dec 1 st at neck edge every other WS row 5 (6, 7, 7, 8) times— 19 (21, 23, 25, 27) sts. Work even until front is same length as back to end of shoulder. Place shoulder sts on holder.

**Right shoulder:** Work as for left shoulder, reversing shaping.

Join front to back at shoulders using 3-needle BO (see page 92).

## NECK

Using 16" circ needle, A, and beg at right back, PU 4 sts down right back, K20 (22, 24, 26, 28) from back neck holder, PU 4 sts up left back, PU 16 (18, 20, 22, 24) sts down left front, K10 from front neck holder, PU 16 sts up right front, pm—70 (76, 82, 88, 94) sts.

Purl 6 rnds. BO loosely.

## SLEEVES

With A and smaller needles, CO 46 (46, 52, 52, 58) sts. Work border as for back. Rest of sleeve is worked in St st and darker color on larger needles.

Inc 1 st at each side every 5 rows 15 (15, 14, 14, 14) times—76 (76, 80, 84, 86) sts.

Work 1 (5, 10, 10, 12) rows even or until desired length to underarm.

BO 10 sts at beg of next 2 rows—56 (56, 60, 64, 66) sts.

BO 2 sts at beg of next 10 rows—36 (36, 40, 44, 46) sts.

BO all sts.

## FINISHING

Sew sleeve into armhole, matching center top of sleeve to shoulder seam.

Sew sleeve and side seams.

Weave in ends.

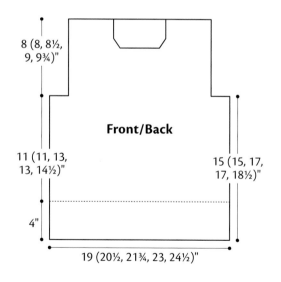

8 (8, 8½, 9, 9¾)"

**Front/Back**

11 (11, 13, 13, 14½)"

15 (15, 17, 17, 18½)"

4"

19 (20½, 21¾, 23, 24½)"

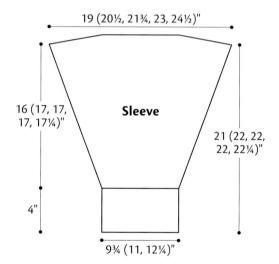

19 (20½, 21¾, 23, 24½)"

16 (17, 17, 17, 17¼)"

**Sleeve**

21 (22, 22, 22, 22¼)"

4"

9¾ (11, 12¼)"

**I** learned a few things while knitting this sweater. First, splice your yarn rather than tying a knot for a gradual color transition. Second, if you come to a knot in this yarn, the next length will most likely not be the same color as before; therefore, you have to find the correct color within the skein and splice it there. Finally, when adding a new skein, look for the same color within the skein. This yarn gradually goes into stripes of different colors, so by not tying in the same color, you lose this beautiful effect.

Skill Level: Intermediate ■■■□

## FINISHED MEASUREMENTS

**Bust:** 40 (42, 44)"

**Length:** 19 (20¾, 22¼)"

**Sleeve length:** 17 (16, 15)"

## MATERIALS

7 (8, 9) skeins* of Paint Box from Knit One, Crochet Too (100% wool; 1¾ oz/50 g; 100 yds/92 m), color 16, Pansy (4)

US 7 (4.5 mm) needles or size needed to obtain gauge

US 6 (4 mm) 16" and 24" circular needles

Stitch holders

*You may want to buy an additional skein or two for splicing at joins.*

## GAUGE

18 sts and 33 rows = 4" in welt patt with larger needles

## WELT PATTERN

**Row 1 (RS):** Knit.

**Row 2:** Purl.

**Row 3:** Knit.

**Row 4:** Purl.

**Rows 5–8:** Knit.

Rep these 8 rows for patt.

## LEFT SLEEVE

This sweater is knit from side to side, starting at the left cuff.

Using size 6, 24" circular needles, CO 48 (52, 56) sts. Work the foll 2 rows twice:

>    **Row 1 (RS):** Purl.

>    **Row 2:** Knit.

Change to size 7 needles and work in welt patt, inc 1 st at each side every 8 rows 15 (14, 13) times—78 (80, 82) sts.

Work rows 1–6 of patt once more.

**Rows 7 and 8:** CO 47 (53, 59) sts, knit to end of row—172 (186, 200) sts.

Work the 8-row patt rep 6 times. Work rows 1 and 2 once more.

### Divide for Neck

**Next row (patt row 3):** K86 (93, 100) for back and place on holder.

The rem 86 (93, 100) sts will be worked for front.

## FRONT

**Cont in patt row 3:** BO 5 (7, 9) sts for neck opening, knit to end of row.

Working in patt, BO 1 st at beg of next 6 RS rows.

Work patt row 8 (WS).

Rep the 8-row patt once; work rows 1–6 once more.

Inc 1 st at beg of next 6 RS rows. Work 1 WS row.

CO 5 (7, 9) sts. Break yarn and place sts on a spare needle.

## BACK

Attach yarn at neck edge on WS and place sts from holder back on needle.

Work rows 3–8 of patt, then work the 8-row patt rep 6 times.

Work patt rows 1 and 2.

Join back to front on patt row 3, working front sts from spare needle. Then work patt rows 4–8.

Work patt rows 1–2.

BO 47 (53, 59) sts at beg of next 2 rows.

Work even for patt rows 5–7.

## RIGHT SLEEVE

Begin on row 8. Work in patt, dec 1 st at each side of sleeve every 8 rows 15 (14, 13) times—48 (52, 56) sts. Work rows 1–5 of patt.

Change to size 6, 24" circular needle and work the foll 2 rows twice:

   **Row 1 (WS):** Knit.

   **Row 2:** Purl.

BO loosely.

## FINISHING

**Neck:** With size 6, 16" circ needle, RS facing, and beg at right shoulder, PU approx 70 (74, 76) sts around neck. Pm and join sts. Purl 6 rnds. BO loosely.

Sew side seams and sleeve seams.

**Bottom edge:** With size 6, 24" circ needle, PU approx 175 (185, 195) sts around bottom. Purl 6 rnds. BO very loosely.

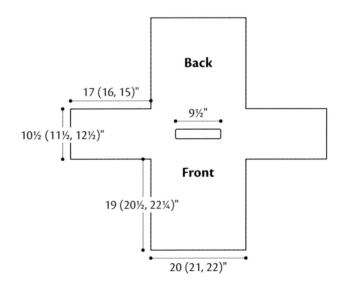

**M**urano, a beautiful island just north of Venice, is famous for its long tradition of glassmaking. It's also the name of this softly striping yarn. Why? I have no earthly idea, but when I was riding the vaporetto (a bus that is a boat) to Murano while in Venice in December, I would have loved to cuddle up in this sweater.

Skill Level: Intermediate ◼◼◼◻

## FINISHED MEASUREMENTS

**Bust:** 37 (40, 42, 45, 46, 48)"

**Length:** 27¼ (27¾, 28, 28½, 29, 31)"

**Length to underarm:** 18"

**Sleeve length to underarm:** 17 (17, 17½, 18, 18½, 19)"

## MATERIALS

4 (5, 5, 6, 6, 6) skeins of Murano by Austermann, (51% virgin wool/49% acrylic; 5¼ oz/150 g; 260 yds/240 m), color 009 (gold/purple/multi)

US 10 (6 mm) 16" and 29" circular needles or size needed to obtain gauge

US 10 (6 mm) double-pointed needles

US 8 (5 mm) 16" and 29" circular needles

US 8 (5 mm) double-pointed needles

K/10½ (6.5 mm) crochet hook

Stitch holders

Stitch markers

7 (7, 7, 8, 8, 9) silver Celtic knot buttons, ¾" diameter (from Black Water Abbey Yarns; see "Resources" on page 96)

## GAUGE

13 sts and 19¼ rows = 4" in St st with larger needles

## STOCKINETTE STITCH

**Worked back and forth:** Knit the RS rows; purl the WS rows.

**Worked in the round:** Knit every rnd.

## GARTER STITCH

**Worked back and forth:** Knit all rows.

**Worked in the round:** Purl 1 rnd; knit 1 rnd.

## SPECIAL ABBREVIATIONS

**CE (chain edge):** Wyif sl 1 pw, return yarn to back of work between needles.

## BODY

The sweater body is worked back and forth on a 29" circular needle.

With smaller needles, CO 116 (124, 132, 140, 144, 152) sts for lower border. The first row is the WS side.

Rep the foll row 7 times, inc 5 sts evenly spaced in the last row: CE, knit to end—121, (129, 137, 145, 149, 157) sts.

Change to larger needles.

**Row 1 (RS):** CE, knit.

**Row 2:** CE, K2, purl to last 3 sts, K3.

Rep rows 1 and 2 until entire piece measures 18" or desired length to armhole, ending with a completed WS row.

**Divide for underarms:** Cont working center front edging on first 3 sts and last 3 sts of every row. AT THE SAME TIME, work 24 (26, 28, 30, 31, 33) sts and place on a holder for right front. BO next 10 sts for underarm; work 53 (57, 61, 65, 67, 71) sts and place on holder for back. BO next 10 sts for underarm; work rem 24 (26, 28, 30, 31, 33) sts and place on holder for left front.

## SLEEVES

Sleeves are worked in the round. Beg on dpns, change to 16" circ needle when possible.

CO 33 (35, 35, 35, 39, 39) sts. Join rnd and pm.

**Rnd 1:** Purl.

**Rnd 2:** Knit.

Work these 2 rnds a total of 3 times.

Work rnd 1, inc 5 sts evenly spaced—38 (40, 40, 40, 44, 44) sts.

Change to larger needles. Work in St st for 6 rnds.

**Work incs as foll:**

**Rnd 1:** K2, M1, knit to last 2 sts, M1, K2.

**Rnds 2–6:** Work in St st.

Work these 6 rnds a total of 7 (7, 8, 9, 10, 11) times—52 (54, 56, 58, 60, 62) sts.

Work even in St st until sleeve measures 17 (17, 17½, 18, 18½, 19)".

BO 5 sts at beg of rnd and 5 sts at end of rnd—42 (44, 46, 48, 50, 52) sts.

Place sts on holder.

## YOKE

With RS facing and cont with center front edging, return sts of right front, 1 sleeve, back, 1 sleeve, and left front from holders to larger needle—185 (197, 209, 221, 229, 241) sts. Work 15 (17, 19, 21, 23, 25) rows of St st, inc or dec sts (as needed) on last row to get 183 (195, 207, 219, 231, 243) sts.

**First dec row:** CE, K3, K2tog, *K4, K2tog , rep from * to last 3 sts, K3—30 (32, 34, 36, 38, 40) sts decreased for a total of 153 (163, 173, 183, 193, 203) sts.

Work 9 rows, inc or dec evenly spaced on last row to get 153 (159, 171, 177, 189, 195) sts.

**Second dec row:** CE, K3, K2tog, *K4, K2tog , rep from * to last 3 sts, K3—25 (26, 28, 29, 31, 32) sts dec for a total of 128 (133, 143, 148, 158, 163) sts.

Work 7 rows, inc or dec evenly spaced on last row for a total of 128 (132, 144, 152, 160, 160) sts.

**Third dec row:** CE, K2, K2tog, *K2, K2tog, rep from * to last 3 sts, K3—31 (32, 35, 37, 39, 39) sts dec for a total of 97 (100, 109, 115, 121, 121) sts.

Work 3 rows, inc or dec evenly spaced on last row for a total of 96 (99, 108, 111, 120, 120) sts.

**Fourth dec row:** CE, K2, *K1, K2tog, rep from * to last 3 sts, K3—30 (31, 34, 35, 38, 38) sts dec for a total of 66 (68, 74, 76, 82, 82) sts.

Work 7 rows even.

**Last dec row:** CE, dec 2 (4, 4, 4, 2, 2) sts evenly spaced along back—64 (64, 70, 72, 80, 80) sts.

## NECKBAND AND HOOD

Change to 16" or 29" size 8 circ needle and work foll row back and forth until hood measures 9½ (9¾, 10, 10, 10½, 10¾)", ending with a completed WS row: CE, knit.

Place half the sts on one needle; the other half on another needle. Holding RS to RS, use 3-needle BO (see page 92) to join top of hood.

## FINISHING

Sew underarm seams.

Starting at bottom edge, sc along right front, all around hood, and down left front. Ch 1, turn. Sc all around, making 7 (7, 7, 8, 8, 9) buttonholes evenly spaced on right front band by chaining desired number of sts to accommodate buttons.

Sew on buttons.

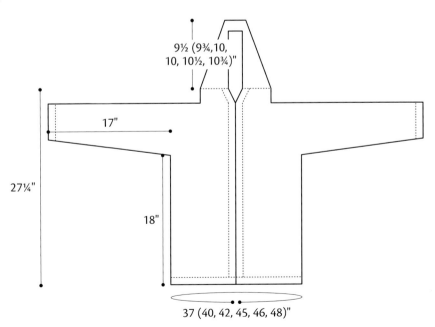

9½ (9¾,10, 10, 10½, 10¾)"

17"

27¼"

18"

37 (40, 42, 45, 46, 48)"

It's hard to believe that tofu and the beautiful yarn used to knit this garment are both byproducts of soy. Using two colors, knit this little kimono topper to keep you warm and stylish.

Skill Level: Intermediate ◼◼◼◻

## FINISHED MEASUREMENTS

**Bust:** 35 (38, 41, 44)"
**Front length:** 13½ (13½, 14, 14½)"
**Center back length:** 16½ (16½, 17, 17½)"
**Sleeve length to underarm:** 18¾ (18, 17½, 17)"

## MATERIALS

SWS by Patons (70% wool/30% soy; 2¾ oz/80 g; 110 yds/100 m) (4)

    **A:** 5 (6, 6, 7) skeins of color 70128, Natural Blue
    **B:** 5 (6, 6, 7) skeins of color 70130, Natural Navy

US 8 (5 mm) needles or size needed to obtain gauge
Stitch holders
1 outrageous button

## GAUGE

17 sts and 34 rows= 4" in garter stitch

## STOCKINETTE STITCH

Knit RS rows; purl WS rows.

## GARTER STITCH

Knit every row.

## SPECIAL ABBREVIATIONS

**CE (chain edge):** Wyif sl 1 pw, return yarn to back of work between needles.

**Kfb (knit front and back):** Knit into front of st, then into back of st.

## RIGHT FRONT

With A, CO 56 (60, 64, 68) sts.

CE, knit to end 39 times, ending with a completed WS row.

Rep the foll 2 rows until 10 sts rem:

    **Row 1 (RS):** CE, K2tog, knit to last 3 sts, K2tog, K1.

    **Row 2:** CE, knit.

Work the foll 7 rows:

    **Row 1 (RS):** CE, K2tog, knit to last 3 sts, K2tog, K1.

    **Row 2 (buttonhole):** CE, K1, BO 2 sts, K2.

    **Row 3:** CE, K2tog, CO 2 sts, K2tog, K1.

    **Row 4:** CE, knit.

    **Row 5:** CE, K3tog, K1.

    **Row 6:** CE, K2.

    **Row 7:** K3tog; fasten off.

## LEFT FRONT

With B, CO 56 (60, 64, 68) sts. Work as for right front, but do not make a buttonhole.

## RIGHT BACK

With B, CO 56 (60, 64, 68) sts.

**Foundation row (WS):** CE, knit.

Work the foll 2 rows 19 times—75 (79, 83, 87) sts:

> **Row 1:** CE, knit to last 2 sts, Kfb, K1.
>
> **Row 2:** CE, knit.

**Shape back neck:**

> **RS:** BO 5 sts, work to last 2 sts, Kfb, K1.
>
> **WS:** CE, knit—71 (75, 79, 83) sts.

Work the foll 2 rows 9 times—80 (84, 88, 92) sts:

> **Row 1:** CE, knit to last 2 sts, Kfb, K1.
>
> **Row 2:** CE, knit.

Work the foll 2 rows 5 times—75 (79, 83, 87) sts:

> **Row 1:** CE, knit to last 3 sts, K2tog, K1.
>
> **Row 2:** CE, knit.

Place sts on a holder.

## LEFT BACK

With A, CO 56 (60, 64, 68) sts.

**Foundation row (WS):** CE, knit.

Work the foll 2 rows 19 times—75 (79, 83, 87) sts.

> **Row 1:** CE, Kfb, knit to end of row.

**Row 2:** CE, knit. On last rep of this row, BO 5 sts—71 (75, 79, 83) sts.

Work the foll 2 rows 9 times—80 (84, 88, 92) sts:

> **Row 1:** CE, Kfb, knit to end.
>
> **Row 2:** CE, knit.

Work the foll 2 rows 5 times—75 (79, 83, 87) sts:

> **Row 1:** CE, K2tog, knit to end.
>
> **Row 2:** CE, knit.

Leave sts on needle. With RS to RS, join seam using 3-needle BO (see page 92).

## RIGHT SLEEVE

Count 12 (16, 20, 24) sts up from bottom side seam of left front. With A, PU 44 sts to shoulder seam, PU another 44 sts—88 sts.

Work in St st for 15¾ (15, 14½, 14)" or until 3" from desired length, ending with a completed WS row. Attach B and work 24 rows in garter st. BO from RS in knit.

## LEFT SLEEVE

Work the same as right sleeve, but reverse all colors.

## FINISHING

Sew underarm and side seams.

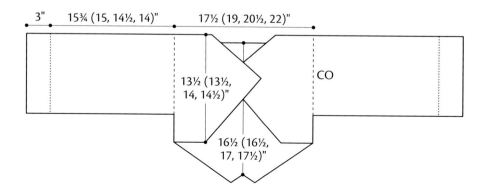

**A**dding different elements of design to self-striping yarn sometimes spices up the works. For this sweater, I added seed-stitch textured check to a basic sweater pattern. The result is interesting to knit and exciting to the eye.

Skill Level: Intermediate ◖■■◗

## FINISHED MEASUREMENTS

**Bust:** 38 (43, 48, 53, 57½)"

**Length:** 20½ (21, 22, 23, 24½)"

**Sleeve Length:** 23¼ (24¼, 24¼, 25, 25¼)"

## MATERIALS

11 (12, 13, 14, 15) skeins of Wooly Stripes by Nashua Handknits (100% wool; 1¾ oz/50 g; 88 yds/80 m), color WS06, Lilac Blossoms ④

US 9 needles (5.5 mm) or size required to obtain gauge

US 7 needles (4.5 mm)

US 7 (4.5 mm) 16" circular needle

G/6 (4.5 mm) crochet hook

Stitch holders

## GAUGE

16¼ sts and 27 rows = 4" in patt with larger needles

## SEED STITCH/STOCKINETTE STITCH BOXES

(Multiple of 10 sts.)

**Row 1 (RS):** *(K1, P1) twice, K1, K5, rep from * to end.

**Row 2:** *P5, (K1, P1) twice, K1, rep from * to end.

**Rows 3–6:** Rep rows 1 and 2 twice.

**Row 7:** *K5, (K1, P1) twice, K1, rep from * to end.

**Row 8:** *(K1, P1) twice, K1, P5, rep from * to end.

**Rows 9–12:** Rep rows 1 and 2 twice.

Rep these 12 rows for patt.

## SEED STITCH

**Row 1:** K1, *P1, K1, rep from * to end.

**Row 2:** Knit the purl sts; purl the knit sts.

Rep these 2 rows for patt.

## FRONT

With smaller needles, CO 77 (87, 97, 107, 117) sts.

Work in seed st for 2".

CO 2 sts at beg of next 2 rows and work rest of rows in seed st.

Change to larger needles and beg patt:

**Row 1:** K1, P1, K1, *K5, (K1, P1) twice, K1, rep from * to last 8 sts, K5, K1, P1, K1.

**Row 2:** K1, P1, K1, *P5, (K1, P1) twice, K1, rep from * to last 8 sts, P5, K1, P1, K1.

**Rows 3–6:** Rep rows 1 and 2 twice.

**Row 7:** K3, *(K1, P1) twice, K1, K5, rep from * to last 8 sts, (K1, P1) twice, K1, K3.

**Row 8:** P3, (K1, P1) twice, K1, P5, rep from * to last 8 sts, (K1, P1) twice, K1, P3.

**Rows 9–12:** Rep rows 7 and 8 twice.

Rep above 12 patt rows until entire piece measures 12½ (12½, 13, 13½, 14½)", ending with a completed WS row.

**Shape armholes:** Cont in patt, BO 4 (4, 6, 7, 8) sts at beg of next 2 rows—73 (83, 89, 97, 105) sts.

**Dec row for armholes:** K3, K2tog, work in patt to last 5 sts, SSK, K3. Work dec row every RS row 5 (5, 6, 7, 7) times—63 (73, 77, 83, 91) sts.

Work even in patt, keeping first 4 sts and last 4 sts of row in St st until armhole measures 5 (5½, 6, 6½, 7)", ending with a completed WS row.

**Shape front neck:** Work 25 (29, 30, 32, 35) sts, place middle 13 (15, 17, 19, 21) sts on a holder for front neck and last 25 (29, 30, 32, 35) sts on holder for right shoulder. Work each side separately.

**Left shoulder:** At beg of next 3 WS rows, BO the foll number of sts to shape neck edge: 3 sts, 2 sts, 2 sts—18 (22, 23, 25, 28) sts. Work 3 rows even.

Dec 1 st at beg of next 3 WS rows—15 (19, 20, 22, 25) sts.

Work even in patt until armhole measures 8 (8½, 9, 9½, 10)", ending with a completed WS row.

**Shape shoulder:** At beg of next 2 RS rows, BO 5 (6, 7, 7, 8) sts.

At beg of next RS row, BO 5 (7, 6, 8, 9) sts.

**Right shoulder:** Attach yarn at neck edge on RS. Work shaping as for left shoulder, working neck shaping on RS rows and shoulder shaping on WS rows.

## BACK

Work as for front, disregarding front neck shaping until armhole measures 8 (8½, 9, 9½, 10)", ending with a completed RS row.

**Next row:** Work 17 (19, 22, 24, 27) sts, place middle 29 (35, 33, 35, 37) sts on a holder for back neck, and last 17 (10, 22, 24, 27) sts on holder for left shoulder. Work each side separately.

**Right shoulder:** BO for shoulders as for front, and AT THE SAME TIME, dec 1 st at neck edge every RS row twice—15 (17, 20, 22, 25) sts.

**Left shoulder:** Attach yarn at neck edge on RS and work as for right shoulder, reversing shaping.

## SLEEVES

With smaller needles, CO 39 (41, 41, 43, 45) sts. Work in seed st as foll for 2": K1, *P1, K1, rep from * to end.

Change to larger needles and establish patt.

**Row 1:** Work first 2 (3, 3, 4, 5) sts in seed st, *K5, (K1, P1) twice, K1* rep from * to * to last 7 (8, 8, 9, 10) sts, K5, work last 2 (3, 3, 4, 5) sts in seed st.

Cont in est patt, inc 1 st at each side every 10 (9, 9, 7, 7) rows 10 (11, 13, 14, 15) times—59 (63, 67, 71, 75) sts. Work even in patt until entire piece measures 17 (17½, 17½, 18, 18)". Work extra sts into patt.

**Shape cap:** BO 4 (4, 6, 7, 8) sts at beg of next 2 rows—51 (55, 55, 57, 59) sts.

**Dec row (RS):** K3, K2tog, work to last 5 sts, SSK, K3.

Work dec row every RS row 17 (18, 18, 19, 20) times, keeping first 3 sts and last 3 sts of each row in St st—17 (19, 19, 19, 19) sts. BO 2 sts at beg of next 2 rows, then 1 st at beg of next 4 rows. BO rem 9 (11, 11, 11, 11) sts.

## FINISHING

Sew shoulder seams.

Sew sleeve into armhole, matching top of sleeve to shoulder seam.

Sew side seams, leaving seed-st border free.

**Neck:** With circ needle and starting at right back shoulder, PU 5 sts down left back, work sts off back neck holder in seed st as est by existing seed-st checks, PU 5 sts up left back to shoulder, PU 18 (20, 22, 24, 26) sts down left front, work sts of front neck holder in seed st as est by existing seed-st checks, PU 17 (19, 21, 23, 25) sts up right front to shoulder—74 (84, 86, 92, 98) sts. Pm.

Work in seed st as est by front and back sts from holders, adjusting sts as necessary to make the transition between picked-up sts and sts from holders. Work in seed st for 2". BO loosely in seed st.

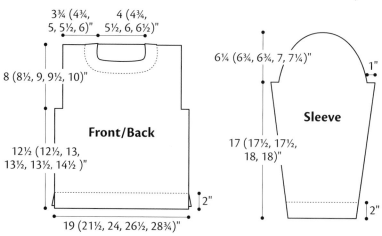

3¾ (4¾, 5, 5½, 6)"  4 (4¾, 5½, 6, 6½)"

8 (8½, 9, 9½, 10)"

**Front/Back**

12½ (12½, 13, 13½, 13½, 14½ )"

19 (21½, 24, 26½, 28¾)"

6¼ (6¾, 6¾, 7, 7¼)"

1"

**Sleeve**

17 (17½, 17½, 18, 18)"

2"

2"

**S**tripes can be made by using different textures as well as different colors. The magic of this yarn is that it changes texture and makes subtle color changes. Don't be fooled by the width of the waist. It stretches!

**Skill Level: Intermediate** ◼◼◼◻

## FINISHED MEASUREMENTS

**To Fit Waist Size:** 26 (28, 30, 32)" (Note: Fabric is very stretchy!)

**Length:** 20"

## MATERIALS

11 (12,13,14) skeins of Boho by Berroco (48% nylon/27% rayon/25% cotton; 1¾ oz/50 g; 98 yds/90 m), color 9276, Raspberries Strawberries (**4**)

US 7 (4.5 mm) 16", 29", and 40" circular needles or size needed to obtain gauge

US 5 (3.75 mm) 16" circular needle

## GAUGE

18 sts and 25 rows = 4" in St st with larger needles

## SKIRT

Change to longer needle when necessary.

**Waistband:** With smaller 16" needle, loosely CO 108 (116, 126, 134). Pm.

Work in K1, P1 rib for 1½", inc 12 (14, 14, 16) sts evenly spaced in last rnd—120 (130, 140, 150) sts.

Change to larger 16" needle and beg patt: *K5, P5, rep from * to end of rnd. Work in this patt until entire piece measures 2".

**First inc rnd:** * K2, M1, K3, P5, rep from * to end—12 (13, 14, 15) sts inc; 132 (143, 154, 165) total sts.

**Next rnds:** K6, P5 around until entire piece measures 3".

**Second inc rnd:** *K3, M1, K3, P5, rep from * to end of rnd—144 (156, 168, 180) sts.

**Next rnds:** K7, P5 around until entire piece measures 5½".

**Third inc rnd:** *K4, M1, K3, P5, rep from * to end of rnd—156 (169, 182, 195) sts.

**Next rnds:** K8, P5 around until entire piece measures 7½".

**Fourth inc rnd:** *K4, M1, K4, P5, rep from * to end of rnd—168 (182, 196, 210) sts.

**Next rnds:** K9, P5 around until entire piece measures 9".

**Fifth inc rnd:** *K5, M1, K4, P5, rep from * to end of rnd—180 (195, 210, 225) sts.

**Next rnds:** K10, P5 around until entire piece measures 10½".

**Sixth inc rnd:** *K5, M1, K5, P5, rep from * to end of rnd—192 (208, 224, 240) sts.

**Next rnds:** K11, P5 around until entire piece measures 11".

**Seventh inc rnd:** *K6, M1, K5, P5, rep from * to end of rnd—204 (221, 238, 255) sts.

**Next rnds:** K12, P5 around until entire piece measures 11½".

**Eighth inc rnd:** *K6, M1, K6, P5, rep from * to end of rnd—216 (234, 252, 270) sts.

**Next rnds:** K13, P5 around until entire piece measures 12".

**Ninth inc rnd:** *K7, M1, K6, P5, rep from * to end of rnd—228 (247, 266, 285) sts.

**Next rnds:** K14, P5 around until entire piece measures 15".

**Tenth inc rnd:** *K7, M1, K7, P5, rep from * to end of rnd—240 (260, 280, 300) sts.

**Next rnds:** K15, P5 around until entire piece measures 17".

**Eleventh inc rnd:** *K8, M1, K7, P5, rep from * to end of rnd—252 (273, 294, 315) sts.

**Next rnds:** K16, P5 around until entire piece measures 18".

**Twelfth inc rnd:** *K8, M1, K8, P5, rep from * to end of rnd—264 (286, 308, 330) sts.

**Next rnds:** K16, P5 around until entire piece measure 19".

**Last inc rnd:** *K9, M1, K8, P5, rep from * to end of rnd—276 (299, 322, 345) sts.

Rep the foll 2 rnds 3 times:

> **Rnd 1:** Knit.
>
> **Rnd 2:** *K18, P5, rep from * to end of rnd.

### RUFFLE

**Rnd 1:** Knit.

**Rnd 2:** Kfb each st—552 (598, 644, 690) sts.

**Rnds 3 and 4:** Knit.

**Rnd 5:** Kfb each st—1,104 (1,196; 1,288; 1,380) sts.

**Rnds 6 and 7:** Knit.

BO all sts.

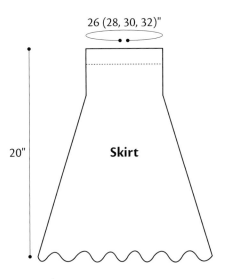

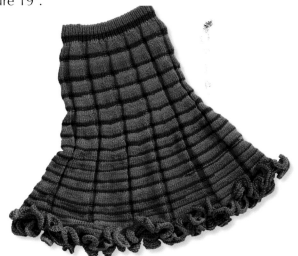

**S**uede yarn by Berroco gives you the wonderful look and feel of suede, but you don't have to kill any cows to get it! You can make the skirt as gathered around the waist as you please, as there's a drawstring to adjust it. It can sit on your hips or on your waist—your choice.

**Skill Level: Intermediate** ◼◼◼◻

## FINISHED MEASUREMENTS

**Waist:** 28" (30, 31½)" (waistband is stretchy)

**Length:** 21"

## MATERIALS

6 (7, 8) skeins of Suede Tri-Color by Berroco (100% nylon; 1¾ oz/50 g; 120 yds/111 m), color 3795 (lime/eggplant/lavender) **4**

US 8 (5 mm) straight and 40" circular needles or size needed to obtain gauge

## GAUGE

18¾ sts and 30 rows = 4" in garter stitch

## SPECIAL ABBREVIATIONS

**CE (chain edge):** Wyif sl 1 pw, return yarn to back of work between needles.

**M1P:** Make 1 purlwise by lifting the running thread between stitches onto the needle and purling into it.

## SKIRT TOP

Using straight needles, CO 57 sts. Work sections A and B 19 (20, 21) times.

### Section A

**Row 1 (WS):** CE, K7, P41, K8.

**Row 2 (RS):** CE, knit.

**Row 3:** Work as for row 1.

**Row 4:** Work as for row 2.

**Row 5:** Work as for row 1.

**Row 6 (make eyelet hole for waistband):** CE, knit to last 5 sts, YO, K2tog, K3.

### Section B

This section creates garter-st short rows for shaping.

**Row 1 (WS):** CE, knit.

**Row 2 (RS):** CE, K36, turn.

**Row 3:** YO, knit to end.

**Row 4:** CE, K26, turn.

**Row 5:** YO, knit to end.

**Row 6:** CE, K16, turn.

**Row 7:** YO, knit to end.

**Row 8:** CE, knit to first YO, knit YO with next st, cont along row, working each YO tog with next st.

**Row 9:** CE, knit.

**Row 10:** CE, knit.

Work rows 1 and 2 of section A once more.

BO all sts and sew side seam.

## RUFFLE

With 40" needle and RS facing, PU into each CE at bottom of skirt—155 (165, 175) sts.

**Rnd 1:** *K4, P1, rep from * around.

**Rnd 2:** *K4, M1P, P1, rep from * around—186 (198, 210) sts.

**Rnd 3:** *K4, P2, rep from * around.

**Rnd 4:** *K4, P2, M1P, rep from * around—217 (231, 245) sts.

**Rnds 5 and 6:** *K4, P3, rep from * around.

**Rnd 7:** *K4, P1, M1P, P2, rep from * around—248 (264, 280) sts.

**Rnds 8–12:** *K4, P1, rep from * around.

**Rnd 13:** *K4, P1, M1P, P2, rep from * around—279 (297, 315) sts.

**Rnds 14–19:** *K4, P5, rep from * around.

**Rnd 20:** *K4, M1P, P5, rep from * around—310 (330, 350) sts.

**Rnds 21–26:** *K4, P6, rep from * around.

**Rnd 27:** Knit.

**Rnd 28:** Purl.

**Rnd 29:** Knit.

**Rnd 30:** Purl.

BO all sts very loosely kw.

## FINISHING

Make a twisted cord for waistline tie. Cut a length of yarn four times the length you wish the cord to be and double it. Tape one end to a table or have someone hold it. Begin twisting the yarn until you see the cord start to kink. Still holding the end taut with one hand, use your other hand to bend the cord in the center, letting the two sides twist around each other. Knot both ends of the cord and weave cord through eyelets in waistband.

Making twisted cord

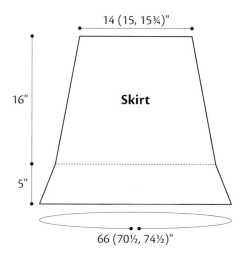

14 (15, 15¾)"

**Skirt**

16"

5"

66 (70½, 74½)"

**W**hat stripe is that ruana? It is the amazing yarn that stripes in texture for you, all softly beautiful, beautifully soft.

Skill Level: Easy ◼◼◻◻

## FINISHED MEASUREMENTS

**Width:** 32"

**Front length:** 12/12"

**Overall length:** 25"

## MATERIALS

8 skeins of Pandora Shadow by Trendsetter Yarns (100% polyamide; 1¾ oz/50 g; 85 yds/90 m), color 1818 (pinkish taupe) **(4)**

US 11 (8 mm) 29" circular needle

## GAUGE

16¾ sts and 20 rows = 4" in Old Shale patt

## OLD SHALE PATTERN

**Row 1 (RS):** CE, knit to end of row.

**Row 2 (WS):** CE, K3, purl to last 4 sts, K4.

**Row 3:** CE, K3, *(K2tog) 3 times, (YO, K1) 6 times, (SSK) 3 times*, rep from * to * to last 4 sts, K4.

**Row 4:** CE, knit.

Rep these 4 rows for patt.

## SPECIAL ABBREVIATIONS

**CE (chain edge):** Wyif sl 1 pw, return yarn to back between needles.

## BACK

CO 134 sts. Work the foll 2 rows 3 times:

**Row 1:** Purl.

**Row 2:** Knit.

Work the 4-row Old Shale patt rep 16 times, then work the foll 4 rows:

**Row 1:** CE, knit.

**Row 2:** CE, K3, P54, K18, P54, K4.

**Row 3:** CE, K3, *(K2tog) 3 times, (YO, K1) 6 times, (SSK) 3 times*, rep from * to * 3 times, K18, **(K2tog) 3 times, (YO, K1) 6 times, (SSK) 3 times**, rep from ** to ** 3 times, K4.

**Row 4 (divide for neck):** CE, K61, BO middle 10 sts, knit rem 62 sts (st left on needle after BO counts as first st of 62).

## RIGHT SIDE

Work the 4-row Old Shale patt rep 16 times, then work 5 rows in garter st, starting with purl row.

BO loosely.

## LEFT SIDE

Attach yarn at neck edge and work as for right side, beg with row 1.

## FINISHING

If desired, sew fronts to back at side seams for 1" or so.

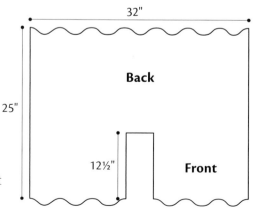

Two rows + two needles + yarn of sunshine = one beautiful shawl. Let this be your first foray into the world of lace knitting!

## MATERIALS

10 skeins of Bernina Le Fibre Nobili by Filatura Cervinia (50% acrylic/45% virgin wool/4% polyamide/1% Lurex; 1¾ oz/50 g; 43 yds/40 m), color 11 (sunshine) **5**

US 15 (10 mm) needles

## GAUGE

10 sts and 12 rows = 4" in lace patt

## SHAWL

CO 49 sts very loosely. Knit 3 rows.

Work the foll 2 rows a total of 53 times:

> **Row 1:** K3, *YO, K2tog, rep from * to last 2 sts, K2.

> **Row 2:** K3, purl to last 3 sts, K3.

Work the foll 2 rows once:

> **Row 1:** K2, *SSK, YO, rep from * to last 3 sts, K3.

> **Row 2:** K3, purl to last 3 sts, K3.

Knit 3 rows. BO very loosely kw from RS.

## FINISHING

Block if desired.

Skill Level: Intermediate ◼◼◼◻

## FINISHED MEASUREMENTS

**Width:** 19"

**Depth at center back:** 26½"

**Length of each side:** 35"

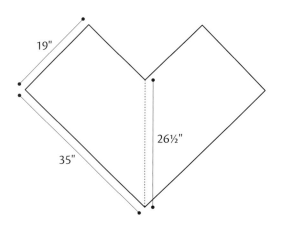

19"

26½"

35"

This easy-to-knit stole is a case in point for letting the yarn make the garment. Three related yarns are worked in garter stitch on the diagonal to make two long rectangles. The magic occurs when the two pieces are sewn together. Chevrons emerge, turning simple garter stitch, decreases, and increases into a romantic beauty.

Skill Level: Intermediate ■■■□

## FINISHED MEASUREMENTS

**Width:** 17"

**Length:** 64"

**Each piece:** 17" x 32"

## MATERIALS

**A:** 2 skeins of Yesterday by Plymouth Yarn Italian Collection (80% mohair/15% wool/5% nylon; 1¾ oz/50 g; 110 yds/102 m), color 1663 (coral) (④)

**B:** 2 skeins of Today by Plymouth Yarn Italian Collection (80% mohair/15% wool/5% nylon; 1¾ oz/50 g; 100 yds/91 m), color 1663 (coral) (④)

**C:** 3 skeins of Tomorrow by Plymouth Yarn Italian Collection (40% nylon/38% mohair/18% acrylic/4% metal; 1¾ oz/50 g; 82 yds/76 m), color 1663 (coral) (④)

US 10½ (6.5 mm) needle or size needed to obtain gauge

## GAUGE

11½ sts and 20 rows = 4" in garter st

## SPECIAL ABBREVIATIONS

**CE (chain edge):** Wyif sl 1 pw, return yarn to back of work between needles.

## PATTERN STITCH

**Row 1(RS):** CE, Kfb, K1—4 sts.

**Row 2 (WS) and all even-numbered rows:** CE, knit.

**Row 3:** CE, K1, Kfb, K1—5 sts.

**Row 5:** CE, Kfb, knit to 2 sts before end of row, Kfb, K1—7 sts.

**Row 7:** CE, Kfb, knit to 3 sts before end of row, K2tog, K1.

**Row 9:** CE, K2tog, knit to last 3 sts, K2tog, K1—2 sts dec.

**Row 10:** CE, knit.

Rep rows 9 and 10 until 5 sts rem.

**Row 11:** CE, K1, K2tog, K1—4 sts.

**Row 12:** CE, knit.

**Row 13:** CE, K2tog, K1—3 sts.

**Row 14:** K3tog.

Fasten off.

## FIRST PIECE

*Make 2 exactly alike.*

With A, CO 3 sts. Knit 1 row.

Mark RS of work when there is enough fabric.

Work rows 1–6 of patt.

Rep rows 5 and 6 until there are 23 sts, ending with a completed row 6 except for the last st. Attach C and work the last st in new color.

Cont with C, work rows 5 and 6 until there are 37 sts, ending with a completed row 6 except for the last st. Attach B and work the last st in new color.

Cont with B, work rows 5 and 6 until there are 51 sts. Attach C as above.

Cont with C, work rows 5 and 6 until there are 61 sts. Attach A as above.

Cont with A, work rows 5 and 6 until there are 69 sts. Attach C as above.

Cont with C, work rows 7 and 8 twice. Attach B as above.

Cont with B, work rows 7 and 8 twice. Attach A as above.

Cont working rows 7 and 8 in the foll color sequence:

    8 rows in A

    10 rows in C

    12 rows in B

    10 rows in A

Work rows 9–10 of the patt in the foll color sequence:

    *4 rows in C

    4 rows in A

    4 rows in C

    4 rows in B*. Rep from * to * 4 times. Work patt rows 11–14 in C. BO all sts.

## FINISHING

Sew pieces together along center back, reversing one piece so that the stripes make a chevron when joined.

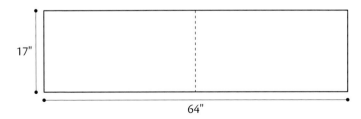

Knitting self-striping yarn in circles makes beautiful concentric rings of color. Add a swirling lace pattern and you have even more interest. I joined pairs of circles with wrong sides together, making this piece totally reversible.

Skill Level: Experienced ◖■ ■ ■ ▬

## FINISHED MEASUREMENTS

**Circle circumference:** 6½"

**Stole width:** 11"

**Stole length:** 60"

## MATERIALS

Karaoke by South West Trading Co. (50% soy silk/ 50% wool; 1¾ oz/50 g, 80 yds/100 m) ⟨4⟩

    **A:** 6 skeins of color 302 (blues)

    **B:** 6 skeins of color 303 (pinks)

US 7 (4.5 mm) double-pointed needles or size needed to obtain gauge

E/4 (3.5 mm) crochet hook

Stitch markers

## GAUGE

18 sts = 4" in St st

## STOCKINETTE STITCH

**In the round:** Knit every rnd.

**Worked back and forth:** Knit on RS; purl on WS.

## CIRCLE

Knit 14 circles using color A and 14 circles using color B. Rows 1–7 are worked back and forth. The rest of the circle is worked in the round.

CO 8 sts, leaving an 8" tail.

**Row 1:** Knit.

**Row 2:** Purl.

**Row 3:** (YO, K1) 8 times—16 sts.

**Row 4:** Purl.

**Row 5:** (YO, K1) 16 times—32 sts.

**Row 6:** (P2, Ptog) 8 times—24 sts.

**Row 7:** (YO, K1, YO, K2tog) 8 times—32 sts. Distribute sts evenly onto dpns.

**Rnd 8:** Knit. This row will join sts into a rnd—place markers after every 4 sts per section.

**Rnd 9:** (YO, K1, YO, K1, YO, K2tog) 8 times.

**Rnd 10:** (Knit to 2 sts before marker, K2tog) 8 times— 5 sts per section.

**Rnd 11:** (YO, K1, YO, K1, YO, knit to 2 sts before marker, K2tog) 8 times.

**Rnd 12:** (Knit to 2 sts before marker, K2tog) 8 times— 6 sts per section.

Rep rnds 11 and 12 until there are 10 sts in each section—80 sts total.

BO loosely. Use the tail to weave through the CO sts; pull up to close center opening. Fasten off.

## JOINING

To join circles, hold 2 circles knit in same color with WS tog and crochet through both circles at the same time. Join yarn A circles using yarn B; join yarn B circles using yarn A.

**Circle 1:** Using 2 circles of the same color, hold WS to WS. Attach yarn, pull up a loop. *Ch 4, skip 1 st, sc in next st, rep from * around entire circle. End with ch 4, sl st into first ch-4 loops.

**Joining circle 2 to circle 1:** Work as for circle 1 for a few ch-4 loops, then begin to attach to circle 1 as foll: *Ch 4, sl st through ch-4 loop on circle 1, ch 4, skip 1 st, sc through next st on circle 2* , rep from * to * 5 times, *ch 4, skip 1 st, sc into next st on circle 2*, rep from * to * for rest of circle. End with ch 4, sl st through first ch 4.

**Joining circle 3 to circles 1 and 2:** Work as for circle 1 for a few loops, *ch 4, sl st into the 7th loop on circle 2, ch 4, skip 1 st, sc into next st on circle 3*, rep from * to * 5 times, *ch 4, skip 1 st, sc into next st on circle 3*, rep from * to * twice, ch 4; starting in 3rd loop from join of circle 1 and circle 2, sl st into loop, ch 4, skip 1 st, sc into next st on circle 3*, rep

from * to * 5 times. *Ch 4, skip 1 st, sc into next st of circle 3, rep from * to end. End with ch 4, sl st into first ch-4 loop.

Cont joining circles in this manner, foll diagram.

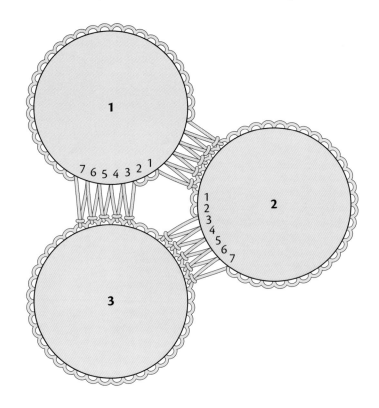

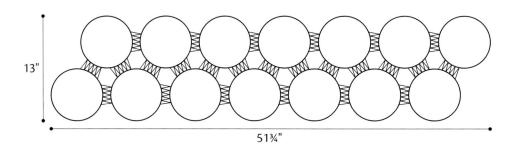

Oh, what a horribly hideous name for a piece so beautiful! This lovely lace pattern is called "Fischgrätlein," which translates to "fish scales." It begins with a few stitches at the neck, working down to the ethereal lace pattern that is mostly composed of air. When you receive compliments on this lovely piece, you can make up a better name for it.

Skill Level: Experienced ■■■▬

## FINISHED MEASUREMENTS

**Width from wing to wing along top:** 60"
**Width from wing to wing along bottom:** 80"
**Center back length:** 18"

## MATERIALS

**A:** 1 skein of Kid Mohair from Louet (70% wool/30% nylon; 1¾ oz/50 g; 490 yds/452 m), color Grey Lavender (**1**)

**B:** 1 skein of Graceful from Yarn Place (100% wool; 3½ oz/100 g; 2,400 yds/2,215 m), color 3617, Sherbert (**1**)

US 8 (5 mm) 40" circular needle

## GAUGE (UNBLOCKED)

20 sts and 28 rows = 4" in fish scales patt, holding 1 strand of each yarn tog

## SHAWL

Using 1 strand of A and 1 strand of B held tog, CO 3 sts.

**Row 1:** Kfb each st—6 sts.

**Row 2:** Knit.

**Row 3:** Kfb each st—12 sts.

**Row 4:** Knit.

**Row 5:** (Kfb) 3 times, (YO, sl 1, K1, psso) twice, (Kfb) 3 times—18 sts.

**Row 6:** K3, P3, (YO, P2tog, P1) twice, P3, K3.

**Row 7:** (Kfb) 3 times, *YO, sl 1, K1, psso, K1, rep from * to last 3 sts, (Kfb) 3 times—6 sts inc; 24 sts.

**Row 8:** K3, P3, *YO, P2tog, P1, rep from * to last 6 sts, P3, K3.

Work rows 7 and 8 a total of 52 times—336 sts.

Knit 2 rows. BO all sts very loosely.

## FINISHING

Weave in ends. Block or steam.

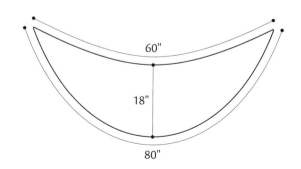

Sometimes the only thing a basic shell needs is a little bit of dash to make it different. This one uses an attractive slip-stitch rib, giving the edgings a three-dimensional quality.

Skill Level: Intermediate ■■■□

## FINISHED MEASUREMENTS

**Bust:** 33 (36½, 40, 43½, 47)"
**Length:** 19 (19, 20, 21, 22½)"

## MATERIALS

5 (6, 7, 8, 9) skeins of Mesa from N.Y. Yarns (72% acrylic/25% wool/3% nylon; 1¾ oz/50 g; 76 yds/70 m), color 6 (bright greens/beige/gray) ⑤

US 10½ (6.5 mm) or size needed to obtain gauge

US 9 (5.5 mm) 16" circular needle

Stitch holders

## GAUGE

14 sts and 24 rows = 4" in St st with larger needles

## STOCKINETTE STITCH

**RS rows:** Knit.

**WS rows:** Purl.

## BORDER PATTERN

**Worked back and forth:**

(Multiple of 4 +1 sts)

**Row 1 (RS):** K1,*P3, K1, rep from * to last 4 sts, P3, K1.

**Row 2 (WS):** P1,* K3, wyif sl 1 st pw, rep from * to last 4 sts, K3, P1.

**Row 3:** K1, *P3, wyib sl 1 st pw, rep from * to last 4 sts, P3, K1.

**Row 4:** Work as for row 2.

**Worked in the round:**

**Rnd 1 (RS):** *P 3, K1, rep from * to end of rnd.

**Rnds 2–4:** *P3, wyib sl 1 st pw, rep from * to end of rnd.

## FRONT

With smaller needle, CO 57 (61, 69, 73, 81) sts.

Work the 4-row border patt (back and forth) twice; work row 1 once more.

**Next row (WS):** Change to larger needles and purl 1 row, inc 1 (3, 1, 3, 1) sts—58 (64, 70, 76, 82) sts.

Work in St st until piece measures 11 (11, 12, 12, 13)", ending with a completed WS row.

**Shape armholes:** At beg of next 2 rows, BO 5 (5, 6, 6, 7) sts—48 (54, 58, 64, 68) sts.

Work the foll 2 rows 6 (8, 9, 10, 11) times—36 (38, 40, 44, 46) sts.

**Row 1:** K3, K2tog, knit to last 5 sts, SSK, K3.

**Row 2:** Purl.

Work even in St st until armhole measures 4½ (4½, 4½, 5½, 6 )", ending with a completed WS row.

**Shape neck (RS):** K14 (14, 15, 16, 17), place middle 8 (10, 10, 12, 12) sts on holder for front neck and last 14 (14, 15, 16, 17) sts on holder or spare needle for right side of neck.

**Left side:** BO 2 sts at beg of next 2 WS rows—10 (10, 11, 12, 13) sts.

Dec 1 st at beg of next 4 (4, 4, 5, 6) WS rows—6 (6, 7, 7, 7) sts.

Work even until armhole measures 8 (8, 8, 9, 9¾)", ending with a completed RS row.

**Shape shoulders (WS):** Purl 4, wrap the fifth stitch, turn, and work back. Purl 2 sts, wrap the third stitch, turn, and work back. Work last row, hiding wraps (see "Short-Row Shaping" on page 92 for more details on wrapping, turning, and hiding wraps). Place sts on holder.

**Right side:** Attach yarn at neck edge. Work neck shaping as for left side, but work shaping on RS rows.

Shape shoulders as for left side, but beg on RS row. Work 1 row after all wraps are hidden.

## BACK

Work as for front, disregarding neck shaping, until back measures same as front to beg of shoulder shaping, ending with a completed WS row—36 (38, 40, 44, 46) sts.

With RS facing, work armhole shaping as for front—36 (38, 40, 44, 46) sts.

Work even until back measures same as front to beg of shoulder shaping, ending with a completed WS row.

**Shape shoulders:** Work right shoulder same as for left front shoulder.

Place middle 24 (26, 26, 30, 32) sts on holder for back neck.

On RS, attach yarn to left shoulder at neck edge. Work left shoulder same as for right front shoulder.

## FINISHING

Join shoulders using 3-needle BO (see page 92).

**Neck:** With smaller (circ) needle, start at right back neck with RS facing. PU 6 sts down right back, K24 (26, 26, 30, 32) from back neck holder, dec 0 (0, 0, 2, 2) sts evenly spaced, PU 6 sts up left back, PU 18 (18, 18, 18, 19) sts down left front, K8 (10, 10, 12, 12) from front holder, PU 18 (18, 18, 18, 19) sts up right front, pm—80 (84, 84, 88, 92) sts. Work border patt in the rnd for 5 rnds. BO loosely in patt.

Sew side seams.

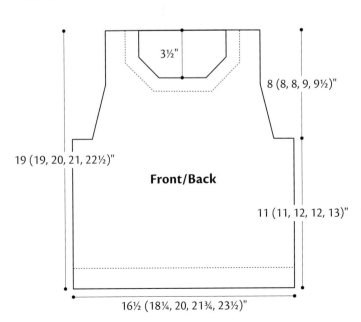

**W**orked from the neck down with a wonderful little swirled yoke, this top is bright and snappy. It's a melody of rainbow and texture.

Skill Level: Intermediate ◖■■▢

## FINISHED MEASUREMENTS

**Bust:** 33 (34, 35, 36, 37)"

**Length:** 18½ (18½, 19½, 19½, 20½)"

## MATERIALS

2 (2, 2, 3, 3) skeins of Cool Stuff from Prism Arts Inc. (rayon, cotton, nylon, polyester, silk; 6–8 oz/168–224 g; 300 yds/277 m), color Cantina (**4**)

US 9 (5.5 mm) 16" and 24" circular needles or size needed to obtain gauge

Stitch holders

Stitch markers

## GAUGE

16½ sts and 19 rows = 4" in St st

## STOCKINETTE STITCH

**Worked back and forth:** Knit on the RS; purl on the WS.

**In the round:** Knit every rnd.

## YOKE

With 16" needle, CO 80 (88, 96, 104, 112) sts, pm after each group of 10 (11, 12, 13, 14) sts. Place a different colored marker at end of rnd.

**Rnd 1:** Purl.

**Rnd 2:** Knit.

**Rnd 3:** Purl.

**Rnd 4:** *(YO, K1) twice, YO, knit to 2 sts before marker, K2tog*, rep from * to * for each section.

**Rnd 5:** *Knit to 2 sts before marker, K2tog*, rep from * to * for each section.

Work rnds 4 and 5 a total of 9 times and then work rnd 4 once more—21 (22, 23, 24, 25) sts in each section; 168 (176, 184, 192, 200) sts total.

**Next rnd:** *Purl to 2 sts before marker, P2tog*, rep from * to * for each section—20 (21, 22, 23, 24) sts in each section; 160 (168, 176, 184, 192) sts total.

Knit 1 rnd, purl 1 rnd.

**Divide for front and back:** BO 40 (42, 44, 46, 48) sts, K40 (42, 44, 46, 48) for front, BO 40 (42, 44, 46, 48) sts, K40 (42, 44, 46, 48) for back.

Place 40 (42, 44, 46, 48) front sts on holder.

## BACK

**Row 1 (WS):** K3, purl to last 3 sts, K3.

**Row 2 (RS):** K3, YO, knit to last 3 sts, YO, K3—42 sts.

Rep rows 1 and 2 three more times—48 (50, 52, 54, 56) sts.

Place these sts on holder.

## FRONT

Place 40 (42, 44, 46, 48) front sts on needle and work as for back.

## JOINING FRONT AND BACK

Change to 24" needle and CO 10 sts, knit across 48 (50, 52, 54, 56) sts of front, CO 20 sts, knit across 48 (50, 52, 54, 56) sts of back, CO 10 sts, pm—136 (140, 144, 148, 152) sts.

Rep the foll 2 rnds 3 times:

> **Rnd 1:** P13, K42 (44, 46, 48, 50), P26, K42 (44, 46, 48, 50), P13.
>
> **Rnd 2:** Knit.

Work even in St st until piece measures 11 (11, 12, 12, 13)" or desired length from armhole.

## BOTTOM BORDER

Work 6 rnds of garter stitch, beg with purl rnd. BO all sts very loosely in knit.

## FINISHING

Weave in ends.

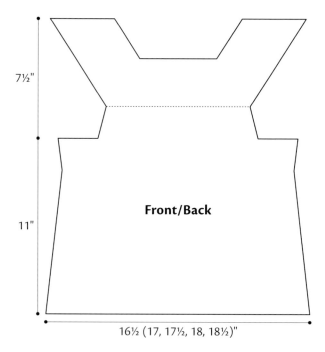

Front/Back

7½"

11"

16½ (17, 17½, 18, 18½)"

*Tutti* is an Italian musical term which means "all together." It also reminds me of a tutti-frutti dessert, which I imagine as a bunch of different fruits all some-how combined together—hopefully with some ice cream thrown in. The colors in this yarn remind me of that delicious dessert.

Skill Level: Intermediate ●■■◻

## FINISHED MEASUREMENTS

Bust: 32 (35, 39, 41, 45, 48½)"

Length: 19¼ (19¼, 19¼, 19¼, 20¼, 20¼)"

Length of side seam: 11 (11, 11, 11, 12, 12)"

## MATERIALS

5 (5, 6, 6, 7, 8) skeins of Bella Colour from Plymouth Yarn Italian Collection (55% cotton/45% acrylic; 1¾ oz/50 g; 104 yds/96 m), color 16 (pastels) 🌀**4**

US 9 (5.5 mm) needles or size needed to obtain gauge

Stitch markers

## GAUGE

20 sts and 27½ rows = 4" in St st

## SPECIAL ABBREVIATIONS

**CE (chain edge):** Wyif sl 1 pw, return yarn to back of work between needles.

## BACK AND FRONT

*Make 2, working from top down.*

CO 28 (32, 36, 40, 44, 48) sts, pm, CO 1 st, pm, CO 28 (32, 36, 40, 44, 48) sts—57 (65, 73, 81, 89, 97) sts.

**Row 1 (WS):** CE, knit.

**Row 2:** CE, K2tog, knit to marker, YO, knit st between markers, YO, knit to last 3 sts, SSK, K1.

**Row 3:** CE, knit to marker, purl st between markers, knit to end.

**Row 4:** Work as for row 2.

**Row 5:** Work as for row 3.

Work the foll 2 rows until side edge of piece along chain edge measures 8¼", ending with a completed row 2:

> **Row 1:** CE, K2tog, knit to marker, YO, K1, YO, knit to last 3 sts, SSK, K1.
>
> **Row 2:** CE, K2, purl to last 3 sts, K3.

**Shape armholes:** CO 11 (11, 11, 11, 12, 12) sts at beg of next 2 rows—79 (87, 95, 103, 113, 121) sts.

Work the foll 6 rows:

> **Row 1:** CE, K2tog, knit to marker, YO, K1, YO, knit to last 3 sts, SSK, K1.
>
> **Row 2:** CE, K13 (13, 13, 13, 14, 14), purl to last 14 (14, 14, 14, 15, 15) sts, K14 (14, 14, 14, 15, 15).

**Row 3:** Work as for row 1.

**Row 4:** CE, K12 (12, 12, 12, 13, 13), purl to last 13 (13, 13, 13, 14, 14) sts, K13 (13, 13, 13, 14, 14).

**Row 5:** Work as for row 1.

**Row 6:** CE, K11 (11, 11, 11, 12, 12), purl to last 12 (12, 12, 12, 13, 13) sts, K12 (12, 12, 12, 13, 13).

Work the foll 2 rows until piece measures 11 (11, 11, 11, 12, 12)" from beg of armhole, ending with a completed row 2.

**Row 1:** CE, K2tog, knit to marker, YO, K1, YO, knit to last 3 sts, SSK, K1.

**Row 2:** CE, K2, purl to last 3 sts, K3.

## BOTTOM BORDER

**Row 1:** CE, K2tog, knit to marker, YO, K1, YO, knit to last 3 sts, SSK, K1.

**Row 2:** CE, knit to middle st, purl middle st, knit to end of row.

Work the prev 2 rows twice more (6 rows total).

BO very loosely in knit from RS.

## FINISHING

Sew side seams. Join shoulders with just a few sts.

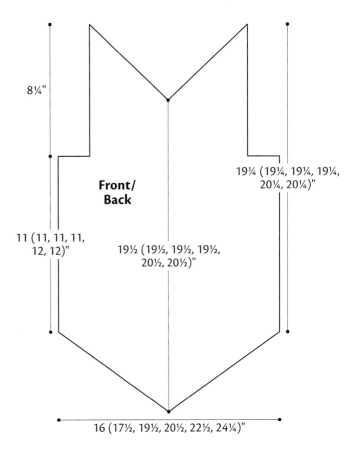

8¼"

**Front/ Back**

11 (11, 11, 11, 12, 12)"

19¼ (19¼, 19¼, 19¼, 20¼, 20¼)"

19½ (19½, 19½, 19½, 20½, 20½)"

16 (17½, 19½, 20½, 22½, 24¼)"

**P**apa Bear, Mama Bear, and Baby Bear can now each have their own bowl, but they won't want to eat porridge from these! The stripes circle around these bowls in beautiful sequences, and felting makes them sturdy containers. Nest them, or use them separately. Make sure to look at the bottoms, as they are incredible concentric circles in Howard Johnson colors.

Skill Level: Intermediate ■■■□

## FINISHED MEASUREMENTS

*Unfelted:*

**Circumference at widest part:** 25 (34, 42½)"

**Height:** 4"

*After felting:*

**Base diameter:** 5 (8, 10)"

**Height:** 3"

## MATERIALS

6 skeins of Loft Zitron from Skacel Collection (100% wool; 1¾ oz /50 g; 109 yds/100 m), color 906 (orange/turquoise) ⑤

US 10½ (6.5 mm) 16" circular needle or size needed to obtain gauge

US 10½ (6.5 mm) double-pointed needles

## GAUGE

18 sts and 22 rows = 4" in St st

## STOCKINETTE STITCH

Knit every rnd.

## BOTTOM BASE

*For all rounds, rep from * to end of rnd.*

CO 80 (120, 160) sts. Pm and join into rnd. Knit 1 starting rnd.

**Rnd 1:** *K8 (13, 18), K2tog.

**Rnd 2 and all even-numbered rnds:** Knit.

**Rnd 3:** *K7 (12, 17), K2tog.

**Rnd 5:** *K6 (11, 16), K2tog.

**Rnd 7:** *K5 (10, 15), K2tog.

**Rnd 9:** *K4 (9, 14), K2tog.

**Rnd 11:** *K3 (8, 13), K2tog.

**Rnd 13:** *K2 (7, 12), K2tog.

**Rnd 15:** *K1 (6, 11), K2tog.

**Rnd 17 (for Small only):** *K2tog.

**Next rnds (for Medium and Large only):** Cont in above manner until 2 sts rem in each section. K2tog in each section.

Fasten off by running yarn through all sts and pulling tight.

## SIDES

PU 80 (120, 160) sts around circumference of circle. Purl 1 rnd; knit 2 rnds.

Work the foll shaping rnds, knitting 2 rnds between each one.

**Rnd 1:** *K10 (15, 20), inc 1, rep from * 8 times—88 (128, 168) sts.

**Rnds 2 and 3:** Knit.

**Rnd 4:** *K11 (16, 21), inc 1, rep from * 8 times—96 (136, 176) sts.

**Rnds 5 and 6:** Knit.

**Rnd 7:** *K12 (17, 22), inc 1, rep from * 8 times—104 (144, 184) sts.

**Rnds 8 and 9:** Knit.

**Rnd 10:** *K13 (18, 23), inc 1, rep from * 8 times—112 (152, 192) sts.

**Rnds 11 and 12:** Knit.

**Rnd 13:** *K12 (17, 22), K2tog, rep from * 8 times—104 (144, 184) sts.

**Rnds 14 and 15:** Knit.

**Rnd 16:** *K11 (16, 21), K2tog, rep from * 8 times—96 (136, 176) sts.

**Rnds 17 and 18:** Knit.

**Rnd 19:** *K10 (15, 20), K2tog, rep from * 8 times—88 (128, 168) sts.

**Rnds 20 and 21:** Knit.

**Rnd 22:** *K9 (14, 19), K2tog, rep from * 8 times—80 (120, 160) sts.

Work applied I-cord around top of bowl as foll:

CO 3 sts onto LH needle.

K2, K2tog, *sl 3 sts pw to LH needle, K2, K2tog, rep from * until all sts are used up. Sew the 3 live slipped sts to the beg of the I-cord.

## FINISHING

Felt bowls, referring to "Felting" on page 90.

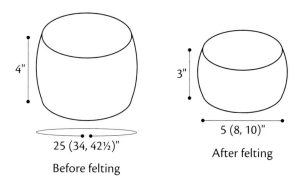

4"

25 (34, 42½)"

Before felting

3"

5 (8, 10)"

After felting

**M**odular items fascinate me, and a bag is the perfect place to experiment. This one starts with the strap. Then the eight-section circle is picked up around the strap and knit toward the center. The result is amazing concentric striped circles. Add a little flap and a pretty button, and you've got a cute little fashion accessory.

Skill Level: Intermediate ■■■▢

## FINISHED MEASUREMENTS

**Width:** 11½"

**Height:** 10"

## MATERIALS

3 skeins of Mesa from N.Y. Yarns (72% acrylic/25% wool/3% nylon; 1¾ oz/50 g; 76 yds/70 m), color 10, Denim ④

US 10½ (6.5 mm) 16" circular needles or size needed to obtain gauge

US 10½ (6.5 mm) double-pointed needles

One 1"-diameter button

Crochet hook for casting on

## GAUGE

16 sts and 20 rows = 4" in St st

## GARTER STITCH

Knit every row.

## STOCKINETTE STITCH IN THE ROUND

Knit every rnd.

## SPECIAL ABBREVIATIONS

**CE (chain edge):** Wyif sl 1 pw, return yarn to back of work between needles.

**CD (central decrease):** Sl 2 sts tog kw, K1, pass slipped sts tog as a unit over the K1.

## STRAP

Provisionally CO 12 sts using dpns (see "Provisional Crochet-Chain Cast On" on page 91). Knit 1 row.

Work the foll row 240 times (120 ridges): CE, knit to end of row.

Graft ends of strap tog as foll: Hold the sts to be joined on two needles with points facing in the same direction and wrong sides tog in your left hand. Thread a tapestry needle with at least 1" of yarn for each st. Attach yarn to back needle and work right to left. Bring yarn through first stitch on front needle pw and leave the st on the needle. Bring the yarn through the first stitch on the back needle kw and leave the st on the needle. *Bring the yarn through the first st on the front needle pw and leave the st on the needle. Bring the yarn through the first stitch on the back needle pw and slip the st off the needle. Bring the yarn through the next st on the back needle kw and leave the st on the needle.* Rep from * to * until 1 st remains on each needle. Bring yarn through st on front needle kw and slip it off. Bring yarn through st on back needle pw and slip it off. See illustration on opposite page.

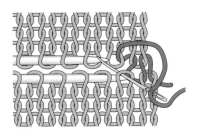

Kitchener stitch

## BAG FRONT AND BACK

*Make 2.*

With circ needle, CO 25 sts. Beg 36 sts to right of strap seam, PU 36 sts (1 st in each CE), to strap seam, PU 35 more sts, and then PU 1 more st, knitting it together with the first CO st—96 sts. Pm for beg and end of rnd. Strap seam is at bag bottom.

**Rnd 1:** Purl.

**Rnd 2:** *K10, K2tog, rep from * to end of rnd.

**Rnd 3 and all odd-numbered rnds:** Knit.

**Rnd 4:** *K9, K2tog, rep from * to end of rnd.

**Rnd 6:** *K8, K2tog, rep from * to end of rnd.

**Rnd 8:** *K7, K2tog, rep from * to end of rnd.

**Rnd 10:** *K6, K2tog, rep from * to end of rnd.

**Rnd 12:** *K5, K2tog, rep from * to end of rnd.

**Rnd 14:** *K4, K2tog, rep from * to end of rnd.

**Rnd 16:** *K3, K2tog, rep from * to end of rnd.

**Rnd 18:** *K2, K2tog, rep from * to end of rnd.

**Rnd 20:** *K1, K2tog, rep from * to end of rnd.

**Rnd 22:** K2tog around.

Fasten off by running yarn through all sts and securing on WS of work.

## FLAP

With RS of bag back facing and starting 2 sts to left of strap, PU 23 sts using single-point needles. Flap is worked back and forth.

**Row 1 (WS):** CE, K10, P1, K11.

**Row 2:** CE, K9, CD, K10.

**Row 3:** CE, K9, P1, K10.

**Row 4:** CE, K8, CD, K9.

**Row 5:** CE, K8, P1, K9.

**Row 6:** CE, K7, CD, K8.

**Row 7:** CE, K7, P1, K8.

Cont in above manner until 3 sts rem, ending with a completed RS row.

Work 3-st I-cord for 3". To make I-cord, K3, slide sts to other end of the dpn and K3. Do not turn between rows. Fasten off and make a loop with I-cord, sewing it to WS of flap.

## FINISHING

Sew button on center of bag front.

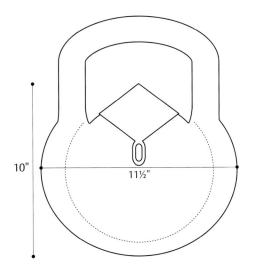

This sturdy basket can hold pounds of yarn, roving, or any such wonderful commodity. Make sure it tips over at opportune moments so your friends can see the beautiful bottom!

Skill Level: Experienced ■■■▶

## FINISHED MEASUREMENTS

*After felting:*

**Base circumference:** approx 17"

**Height:** approx 9"

## MATERIALS

10 skeins of Deluxe Chunky LP by Universal Yarn Inc. (100% wool; 3½ oz/100 g; 120 yds/110 m), color 07 (turquoise/pink) 🧶5

US 11 (8 mm) straight and 19" circular needles

Stitch marker

## GAUGE

12½ sts and 18 rows= 4" in St st

## GARTER STITCH

Knit every row.

## STOCKINETTE STITCH

Knit every rnd.

## SPECIAL ABBREVIATIONS

**CE (chain edge):** Wyif sl 1 pw, return to back of work between needles.

## BASKET BOTTOM

CO 30 sts.

**Row 1 (WS):** Wyib sl first st pw, knit to end of row.

**Row 2 (RS):** CE, knit to 2 sts before end of row. Turn.

**Row 3:** YO, knit to end of row.

**Row 4:** CE, knit to 1 st before YO from previous row. Turn.

**Row 5:** YO, knit to end of row.

Rep rows 4 and 5 until there are 4 sts at beg of row before YO. The sts will be in groups of 2 (st, YO).

**Next row:** CE, K2, turn, YO, K3.

**Last row:** CE, K2, *knit the YO with the next st, rep from * to end of row.

Work 5 more sections as above.

Sew the live sts of last section to CO row of first section.

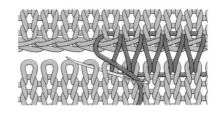

## BOTTOM RIDGE

With circ needle and RS facing, PU 1 st in each of the CE sts around outside of circle. Join and pm.

Knit 8 rnds.

**Form bottom welt:** Insert RH needle into st on LH needle, then into CE st that is on WS of outside of circle. Knit these 2 sts tog. Cont around entire circle in this manner.

Work in St st until piece measures 13" from welt.

Purl 8 rnds.

**Form top welt:** Insert RH needle into st on LH needle, then into ridge on WS directly below first row of purl. Knit these 2 sts tog. Cont around entire circle in this manner.

BO all sts very loosely.

## FINISHING

Weave in all ends.

Felt, referring to "Felting" on page 90.

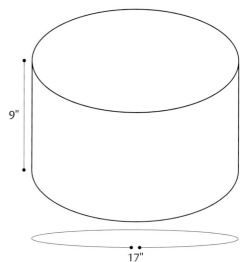

9"

17"

**R**eminiscent of sparkling Amish quilts, the geometric intrigue of this bag, coupled with the random striping of two different-color yarns, makes an eye-catching piece. Sturdy and thick from felting, the bag can be kept closed with a snap at the top if you wish.

Skill Level: Intermediate ◖■■◻

## FINISHED MEASUREMENTS

*Before felting:*

**Width:** 17"

**Height:** 19"

**Total circumference:** 34"

*After felting:*

**Width:** approx 13"

**Height:** approx 11"

**Total circumference:** approx 26"

## MATERIALS

Vero by Wentworth Distributors Ltd (100% wool; 1¾ oz/50 g; 87 yds/80 m):

>   **A:** 5 skeins of color 11 (denim blues) 🧶

>   **B:** 5 skeins of color 14 (ocean) 🧶

US 10½ (6.5 mm) straight and 16" circular needles or size required to obtain gauge

US 10½ (6.5 mm) double-pointed needles

N (9 mm) crochet hook

Spare needle

Stitch markers

## GAUGE

13 sts and 28 rows = 4" in garter st

## GARTER STITCH

**Worked back and forth:** Knit every row; 2 rows = 1 ridge

**Worked in the round:** Purl 1 rnd, knit 1 rnd; 2 rnds = 1 ridge

## FRONT AND BACK

*Make 2.*

Make 2 triangles using yarn A and 2 using yarn B.

With A and straight needles, CO 35 sts.

Work the foll 2 rows until 5 sts rem:

>   **Row 1 (WS):** Knit.

>   **Row 2:** K1, K2tog, knit to last 3 sts, K2tog, K1.

**Next RS row:** K, K3tog, K1.

**Next WS row:** K3.

**Last RS row:** K3tog.

Fasten off.

Sew the triangles together to form a diamond, referring to the illustration for color sequence.

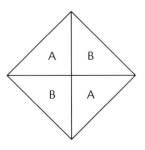

With RS facing, PU 33 sts along one edge of diamond, using color opposite the one used for triangle. Work triangle as above. Rep, picking up and working a triangle along each edge of the center diamond.

## SIDES

With RS facing and using straight needles, PU 40 sts along left edge of bag front using A. Knit 19 rows. Leave sts on spare needle. Using B, work right edge of bag front in same manner.

Repeat for bag back, working 19 rows along both right and left edges of bag back.

Join front to back at sides using 3-needle BO (see page 92).

## TOP

With RS facing, using A and 16" circ needle, PU 109 sts along top edge of bag. Starting with a purl row, work 12 ridges of garter st. BO loosely.

## BOTTOM

With RS facing, using B and 16" circ needle, start in the middle of bag front or back. PU 18 sts, pm, PU 1 st (line of miter), pm, PU 20 sts along side of bag, pm, PU 1 st (line of miter), pm, PU 36 sts along other complete side of bag, pm, PU 1 st (line of miter), pm, PU 20 sts along side of bag, pm, PU 1 st (line of miter), pm, PU 18 sts along front or back. Place different-color marker here to indicate beg and end of rnd.

Beg with a purl rnd, work in garter st for 12 ridges.

**Beg bottom shaping:**

> **Rnd 1:** *Knit to 1 st before first marker, remove markers, sl 1, K2tog, psso, replace markers on each side of resulting st*, rep from * to * for each line of miter, knit to end of rnd.
>
> **Rnd 2:** Purl.

Work these 2 rnds until there are no sts left between lines of miter, changing to dpns when necessary.

Break yarn. Divide rem sts in half on 2 dpns as shown. With RS tog, join using 3-needle BO.

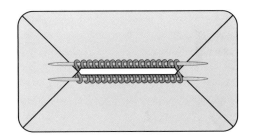

## STRAPS

*Make 2—1 using yarn A and 1 using yarn B.*

I like to crochet my straps, as I find it easier than knitting on such a small number of sts.

Ch 10. Starting in second ch from hook, sc in each chain—9 sc. *Ch 1, turn. Sc in each sc.* Rep from * to * for 26". Fasten off.

Leaving 3" at each end open, sew long sides of strap together. Sew onto bag in desired places.

## CROCHET

**Chain (ch):** Place a slip stitch on hook. Holding hook in right hand and tensioning yarn in left as shown, draw working yarn through slip stitch on hook. Repeat for the desired number of chains.

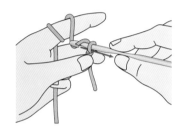

**Single crochet (sc):** *Insert hook under the two top threads of the stitch. Yarn over hook and draw it through the stitch. There are now two loops on hook. Yarn over hook and draw it through both loops on hook. Repeat from * for the desired number of single crochets.

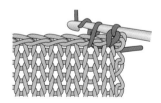

If you can't or don't want to crochet, then you can knit straps as foll:

CO 10 sts and work in garter st for 26". Sew as directed for crocheted straps.

## FINISHING

Felt bag, referring to "Felting" below.

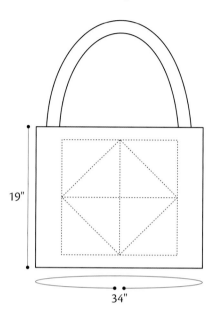

19"

34"

## FELTING

Place the bag or other project in a zippered lingerie bag or a pillowcase secured with a rubber band. Felt in washing machine using hot water and a very small amount of detergent. Check frequently to see how felting is progressing. Depending on the yarn used, a knitted item may felt in as little as 10 minutes with heavy-duty agitation. When the project has felted to desired size, turn washer to rinse and spin cycles to remove detergent and excess water, or rinse and squeeze by hand to prevent creasing. Remove the project from the bag and manipulate it into shape. For slippers, you may want to try them on to make sure they are the right size before allowing to dry. Stuff project with newspaper or plastic bags and let dry.

I am assuming that, as a knitter, you know most of the techniques required to make a sweater. There are a few specific techniques that I call for in individual patterns. These are described below.

## CASTING ON

Casting on is a matter of preference. We most likely use the tried-and-true one that we learned when we first learned to knit. If the pattern doesn't specify a type of cast on, then you may use your favorite method. Some of the patterns in this book, however, call for a specific method. While I cannot stand over you and make you do the called-for method, to get the best results, I strongly recommend you do what I say!

**Long-Tail Cast On:** Draw out about 1½" of yarn for each stitch to be cast on. Make a slipknot on needle. Place yarn in left hand as shown. Bring needle under front strand of thumb loop (it is now between the two loops on thumb), behind and under front strand of forefinger loop, then dip it back between the two strands of thumb loop (under first strand). Let go of the strands on thumb and tighten stitch on needle.

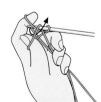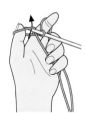

To ball of yarn

To cut end

**Crochet-Chain Cast On:** Use a crochet hook about the same diameter as the needle being used. Place a slipknot on the crochet hook. Hold the crochet hook in your right hand, the knitting needle in your left hand. Hold the working yarn behind the knitting needle. *Place the hook over the needle and draw a loop with the working yarn through the slipknot on the hook. Place working yarn behind needle and repeat from *. For the last stitch, place the loop from the hook onto the needle.

Crochet a chain over top of knitting needle.

**Provisional Crochet-Chain Cast On:** Work as for "Crochet-Chain Cast On" (above), using a smooth waste yarn. When the desired number of stitches are on the needle, chain 3 and fasten off. Tie a knot in the tail to remind you that this is the end to pull out. Proceed to knit with main yarn. When live stitches are needed, pick out the first stitch from the knotted tail end, and then carefully unzip the crochet chain, picking up the live stitches on a needle as they pop out.

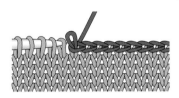

Remove chain one stitch at a time.

**Cable-Edge Cast On:** This cast-on method is used when you need to add stitches to work already in process, such as adding on to the body of a sweater for sleeves. Place a slipknot on the left-hand needle. Insert tip of right needle through the loop on left needle and knit a stitch, placing it on the left needle by dipping the left needle under the stitch. *Insert the right needle between the two stitches and knit a stitch, placing it on the left needle as above. Repeat from *.

Insert needle between
two stitches. Knit a stitch.

Place new stitch
on left needle.

## BINDING OFF

While there are also many methods of binding off, once again, we most likely use the plain old bind off of knit 2, pass the first stitch over the second, knit 1, pass the stitch over, and so on. Providing you do this loosely and neatly, it works just fine. Three-needle bind off is a great method that makes beautifully neat and smooth seams, but can only be used when there are live stitches on the needle.

**Three-Needle Bind Off:** Holding work right side to right side produces an invisible seam; holding work wrong side to wrong side produces a ridge on the right side of the work. Place each set of stitches on a needle with both the points facing the same direction and hold together, one in front, one in back. Insert the

right-hand needle (the third needle) through the first stitch on both needles and knit. Repeat for the second stitch, then pass the first stitch over the second as you would do in a normal bind off. Continue binding off in this manner until all stitches are worked.

Knit together 1 stitch from front
needle and 1 stitch from back needle.

Bind off.

## SHORT-ROW SHAPING

Shoulder shaping for many patterns is often written in the traditional way. The number of stitches for the shoulder is usually divided by three, and the resulting number is bound off at the beginning of three alternate rows. This produces a "stairstep" that some knitters find unsatisfactory. To eliminate this, you can do short-row shaping. Designs that do not have complicated stitch patterns can easily be worked using this method. The technique of wrapping and turning and hiding wraps is explained below. (Note: this type of short-row shaping is also used in the "Short Row 'round the Hat" project on page 30.)

**Wrap and turn on right-side row:** Work the specified number of stitches to where it says "wrap and turn." With yarn in back, slip next stitch purlwise, bring yarn to opposite side of work, slip same stitch back to left needle, and turn, bringing yarn to purl side of work. The wrapped stitch will be on the right needle. Slip first stitch on left needle and work back.

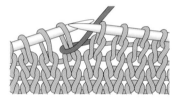

Slip stitch as if to purl. Move yarn to front of work and slip stitch back to left needle.

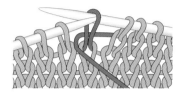

Move yarn to back of work. Turn.

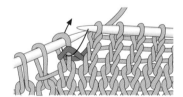

On the final row, knit bar (wrap) and stitch together.

**Wrap and turn on wrong-side row:** Work the specified number of stitches to where it says "wrap and turn." With yarn in front, slip next stitch purlwise, bring yarn to knit side of work, slip same stitch back to left needle, and turn, bringing yarn to purl side of work. The wrapped stitch will be on the right needle. Slip first stitch on left needle and work back.

**Hiding wraps:** On subsequent rows, hide wrapped stitch of previous row by inserting point of right needle under wrap and through wrapped stitch, knitting or purling them together.

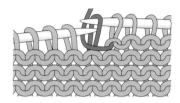

Slip stitch as if to purl. Move yarn to back of work and slip stitch back to left needle.

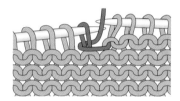

Move yarn toward you. Turn.

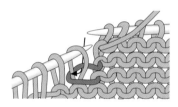

On final row, purl bar (wrap) and stitch together.

**Binding off short-row shaping:** If the garment is made from heavy yarn, you may want the extra stability of a sewn shoulder seam. In that case, bind off all stitches across the row after short-row shaping has been completed, and sew the shoulder seam as usual. If the garment is lightweight, then a three-needle bind off is the perfect finish. After short-row shaping has been completed, put the stitches onto holders and proceed with three-needle bind off.

# ABBREVIATIONS

| | |
|---|---|
| beg | beginning |
| BO | bind off |
| CC | contrasting color |
| CE | chain edge (slip first stitch purlwise, work rest of row) |
| ch | chain |
| circ | circular |
| cn | cable needle |
| CO | cast on |
| cont | continue |
| dec | decrease, decreasing, decreased |
| dpn(s) | double-pointed needle(s) |
| EOR | every other row |
| est | established |
| foll | follows, following |
| inc | increase, increasing |
| K | knit |
| K1tbl | knit 1 stitch through back loop |
| K2tog | knit 2 stitches together |
| K2tog tbl | knit 2 stitches together through back loop |
| K3tog | knit 3 stitches together |
| Kfb | knit into the front and back of a stitch, increasing 1 stitch |
| kw | knitwise |
| LH | left hand |
| lp | loop |
| M1 | make 1 stitch |
| M1P | make 1 stitch purlwise |
| MC | main color |

| | |
|---|---|
| P | purl |
| P1tbl | purl 1 stitch through back loop |
| P2tog tbl | purl 2 stitches together through back loop |
| patt | pattern |
| pm | place marker |
| prev | previous |
| psso | pass slipped stitch(es) over |
| PU | pick up and knit |
| pw | purlwise |
| rem | remains, remaining |
| rep(s) | repeat(s) |
| rev St st | reverse stockinette stitch |
| RH | right hand |
| rnd(s) | round(s) |
| RS | right side |
| sc | single crochet |
| sl | slip |
| sl st | slip stitch |
| SSK | slip 1, slip 1, knit 2 slipped stitches together |
| SSP | slip, slip, purl 2 slipped stitches together |
| st(s) | stitch(es) |
| St st | stockinette stitch |
| tbl | through back loop |
| tog | together |
| wyib | with yarn in back |
| wyif | with yarn in front |
| WS | wrong side |
| YO | yarn over |

## METRIC CONVERSIONS

To easily convert yards to meters or vice versa for calculating how much yarn you'll need for your project, use these handy formulas.

Yards x .91 = meters

Meters x 1.09 = yards

Grams ÷ 28.35 = ounces

Ounces x 28.35 = grams

## SKILL LEVELS

The skill levels assigned to each project in this book are based on the guidelines provided by the Craft Yarn Council of America. Below is a description of what you can expect in a project of each skill level.

■□□□ **Beginner:** Projects for first-time knitters using basic knit and purl stitches. Minimal shaping.

■■□□ **Easy:** Projects using basic stitches, repetitive stitch patterns, and simple color changes. Simple shaping and finishing.

■■■□ **Intermediate:** Projects using a variety of stitches, such as basic cables and lace, simple intarsia, and techniques for double-pointed needles and knitting in the round. Midlevel shaping and finishing.

■■■■ **Experienced:** Projects using advanced techniques and stitches, such as short rows, Fair Isle, more intricate intarsia, cables, lace patterns, and numerous color changes.

| YARN WEIGHTS | | | | | | |
|---|---|---|---|---|---|---|
| **Yarn-Weight Symbol and Category Names** | **Super Fine** 1 | **Fine** 2 | **Light** 3 | **Medium** 4 | **Bulky** 5 | **Super Bulky** 6 |
| **Types of Yarn in Category** | Sock, Fingering, Baby | Sport, Baby | DK, Light Worsted | Worsted, Afghan, Aran | Chunky, Craft, Rug | Bulky, Roving |
| **Knit Gauge Ranges in Stockinette Stitch to 4"** | 27 to 32 sts | 23 to 26 sts | 21 to 24 sts | 16 to 20 sts | 12 to 15 sts | 6 to 11 sts |
| **Recommended Needle in US Size Range** | 1 to 3 | 3 to 5 | 5 to 7 | 7 to 9 | 9 to 11 | 11 and larger |

# RESOURCES

The following yarn companies generously donated their yarns to be used in this book:

**Berroco**
800-343-4948
www.berroco.com

**Spirit of Norway**
866-347-0809
www.spirit-norway.com

**Knit One, Crochet Too, Inc.**
www.knitonecrochettoo.com

**South West Trading Co.**
480-894-1818
www.soysilk.com

**Universal Yarn Inc.**
704-679-3911
www.universalyarn.com

**Skacel Collection**
425-291-9600
www.skacelknitting.com

**Patons**
519-291-3232
www.patonsyarns.com

**Tahki/Stacy Charles, Inc.**
718-326-4433
800-338-YARN
www.tahkistacycharles.com

**Yarn Place**
408-739-7888
www.yarnplace.com

**Louet**
www.louet.com

**Plymouth Yarn Co.**
800-523-8932
www.plymouthyarn.com

**Trendsetter Yarns**
www.trendsetteryarns.com

**Prism Arts, Inc.**
www.prismyarn.com

**Black Water Abbey Yarns**
720-320-1003
www.abbeyyarns.com

**Vero**
Naturally NZ, distributed by
Fiber Trends, Inc.
509-884-8631
www.fibertrends.com

# ABOUT THE AUTHOR

Candace Eisner Strick is an internationally known knitwear designer, teacher, and author. After teaching Suzuki cello for 16 years, she now devotes all her time to knitwear design. She crisscrosses the country and sometimes the Atlantic, teaching knitting. Her new line of yarn, Merging Colors, debuted in April 2006 to rave reviews. She and her husband run their yarn and pattern business, Strickwear, from their home in rural Connecticut. When not knitting, Candace bicycles the back roads and country lanes of Connecticut on her Fuji Ace. This is her fourth book about knitting. She has also written books on quilting and crochet.